T0209782

A

MISSIONARY'S
POINT OF VIEW

WITH TEACHING SECTION

REV. MONIKA G. INTSIFUL

authorHOUSE®

AuthorHouse™
1663 Liberty Drive
Bloomington, IN 47403
www.authorhouse.com
Phone: 1 (800) 839-8640

Published by AuthorHouse 10/22/2019

ISBN: 978-1-7283-3197-3 (sc)
ISBN: 978-1-7283-3196-6 (e)

Print information available on the last page.

This book is printed on acid-free paper.

CONTENTS

PART THREE

Evangelism

Missionary

Last Things

FOREWORD

This book is written for the average person, not from a clinical standpoint, but experiential – what it really is to be missionary. It also includes an instructional portion to be used in evangelism and mission training.

All mission work is to glorify God and to bring honor to His name. The work is to demonstrate the love of Christ. It is not enough to say, "be warm and be filled" because faith without works is dead. (James 2:14-17 NRSV) All in all, God is showing what faithfulness to His commands will accomplish. God has gone before us, and His glory is abounding.

Mission comes with a burning desire to go amidst persecutions. It is a fire shut up in my bones, if I don't do it, I will explode! Missionaries carry with us a sense of urgency, time is of the essence and time is running out. We believe that all humans hunger for God, and that hunger needs to be satisfied. Therefore, we look for new strategies in exhorting churches to step up and make a difference in this world, to the end that all the earth will glorify God.

We also know that God's desire is that none should perish but that all should come to repentance. We know that God's passion is for the lost. We see that in Luke 15 with the parables of the lost coins, the lost sheep and the prodigal son. We understand God's joy at one who has been "found".

Church growth has to be through mission which corresponds with and is sealed with church planting. This mission "field" seriously encompasses Europe and the United States of America. When the Lord told us to go to all nations, making disciples, that meant to all peoples, tribes and tongues. It would be good to follow the steps of African churches who step out in faith and walk in the power of the resurrection by planting churches in places we Westerners would not go. Churches are being planted by Africans in Morocco, Libya and other lands where being Christian is against the law and sometimes punishable by death.

Ministry is not without cost. Trials and persecutions come from without and within. While we suffer slings and arrows in the midst of serving, Scripture reminds us "our present suffering is not worth comparing to the glory to be revealed to us in the future." We truly are a peculiar people, set apart for God's use.

We walk by faith, that one plants, one waters and God gives the increase. We plant or water and are fully confident that God has accomplished what He set up. When I was reading about the great missionary William Sheppard, I saw that for all his efforts and that of his wife, the elders of the Bakuba people never would confess Jesus Christ as Savior, but that their offspring did. This is by patient relationship building. God's work is never in vain.

Psalm 72:18 and 19 declares that God's desire is that He be worshipped and His glory known among all the peoples of the earth. That is the true aim of mission.

Many thanks to Rev. Dr. Camille Still, Director of Religious Education at Omega Baptist Church, Dayton, Ohio for reviewing and giving great advice to Part 3. As a mentor to clergy and the Dean of The Urban Leadership Academy in Dayton, Ohio, I am grateful to her that she would lend her expertise and knowledge in reviewing Part 3 of this document.

PART ONE

LET'S BEGIN

INTRODUCTION

Standing on the shoulders of mission pioneers.

Lott Carey began his missionary career in 1821, and co-founded the nation of Liberia. The missionary convention bearing his name founded mission posts in Siberia in the mid 1800's.

William Colley became a missionary to West Africa in 1875, being sent by the Foreign Mission Board of the Southern Baptist Convention. He is the primary force in the founding of the Baptist Foreign Mission Convention on November 24, 1880. Colley and his wife were appointed as missionaries to West Africa again in 1883 by the BFMC.

William Sheppard went to the Congo in the mid to late 1800's to the fierce and feared Bakuba people. In that day, a black missionary could not go unless a white man went along, and unfortunately, William Sheppard's white companion died a few months after arriving in the Congo. Sheppard worked and toiled with his wife, Lucy Gant and did incredible things including building churches, day schools and translating the bible into the local language. He is responsible for bringing King Leopold of Belgian to the World Court and stopped the Belgian government from their decimating the Congo land.

Beginning in 1878, *Amanda Smith*, became the first black woman international evangelist serving in England, Ireland, Scotland, India and various African countries including Sierra Leon.

Bishop Henry McNeal Turner of the AME Zion church is often recognized as a great political voice and activist for Black freedom in the U. S., and the originator of the back to Africa concept. Research reveals that Bishop Turner is responsible for training and sending many African American missionaries to Sierra Leon, Liberia and South Africa. (He also went) These African American missionaries brought with them the liberating Gospel of Jesus Christ. They were so effective that the South African government threw out the black missionaries because they had the audacity to teach the people that this land was their land. Despite the missionaries' ouster, they came again and again. How awesome a work for the Lord.

The people God has sent me to are wonderful, gracious, loving people, full of the dignity and grace of God Himself. We in the West have to get over ourselves as having the market cornered on spirituality and more particularly the "correct" way of being a Christian.

While we Westerners think we can teach and bless persons in the "third world," in fact, we have so much to learn from our brethren there. We need to shed our superiority complex and be open to the love of God that comes thru the people we come alongside with. In our ill-conceived notions of our superiority we, intentionally or unintentionally, bring into ministry an arrogance that we need to purge. God in most likelihood is using those we serve to bless us and raise us up to be what God has called us to be and, most importantly, in relationship with Him. What I tell people who are going on mission trips is to observe first and listen, before jumping in and imposing our vernacular and traditions. We also should not be so ready to assume that the people don't know God and can't articulate Him in their context and experience.

In spite of us condemning complex interrelationships with ancestors, it is not strange to Scripture that it be so. People honor the ancestors because it is their legacy and teachings upon which they build and maintain their society. It is the same as witnessed in the Old and New Testament writings. The shrines that I have seen in Ghana remember a point in history that is critical to the various societies. It is the same as witnessed in the Old and New Testament writings.

The "West" also has its shrines. We honor the mountain where former presidents of the U. S. are carved, people pray and cry at the "eternal flame" of John F. Kennedy, the Vietnam War Memorial, the Lincoln Memorial, the Washington monument. Yet we have the arrogance and audacity to sneer at and criticize societies who do the same relative to their history. The Scriptures reveal many places where the forefathers erected memorials to remember important events and the intervention of God. The Israelites were cautioned to pray for the ancestors and the Apostle Paul reminds us that a great cloud of many witnesses surrounds us.

Of most importance is to always exalt the name of Jesus the Christ, to give Glory to God and to listen to the directives of the Holy Spirit. To do His will is the only true joy in life.

CHAPTER 1

Lessons Learned "Otherness" is a strange place to be in, as it makes people I know and love, strangers

Mission work is transformational. We are asked to give up all of our personal possessions, to be in discomfort and in need so that others can be blessed by the preached and demonstrated Word of God. We do so not begrudgingly or feeling that we are sacrificing, but we do it joyously and with glad anticipation. This is something not well understood by many persons.

Throughout this walk, I have learned many things. I have learned that I can persevere, and that in all, and in spite of all, I can and should praise the Lord. The people of Ghana don't stop praising Him. Even the school children every day have devotions and prayers. I am grateful that God allows me to see the people as He sees them – well, whole and victorious. Otherwise, my heart would be broken and I would be paralyzed. It is walking not by sight but by faith that brings me through.

God has taught me to be "content in want and content in plenty." When God first gave the assignment, I lived in a nice three-bedroom house with a wonderful yard. I love flower gardening and also had a vegetable and fruit garden in the back. It was my absolute joy to go out and fetch fresh vegetables and fruit, call my grandsons who lived next door and sit back there in the sun having a great lunch with them straight out of the garden. My flowers and shrubs were wonderful. But God said that I needed to give that up for the call. He told me that it was not so much sacrifice as it was that while I am away doing the ministry, having a house would be a burden, source of stress and distraction. God helped me to "dispossess" myself and let these things go. There is a freedom and strength that has come with not being attached to house and home, and yes, even to my flowers.

I have learned to wash my body and to brush my teeth with a small bottle of water. I can wash with the presence of Anansi (tarantula) and hold in my fear. I have learned that I can be flexible if I have to and God told me He has loved me with an everlasting love. I thank God for a cool breeze, for cold water baths, I thank Him for electricity. Even though power outages are a constant in Ghana, when I have had malaria, I asked God for electricity so I can have my feverish body cooled by a fan – He sees to it that there is no power outage the whole time of my recovery. He provides rain when there should be no rain. God is so faithful! Oh, that I would be as faithful to Him!

In times of suffering the effects of some devastating bouts with malaria, God sits down on the bed with me and has a long chat with me, revealing His pleasure and displeasure concerning the conduct of my life, but He always holds me and gives me His wonderful quieting, and reassuring love. At the very occasion of illness sometimes the Holy Spirit swoops down on me and engulfs me, teaching, exhorting, and even laughing with me. I treasure those moments.

When I was young, I lost my way and suffered many hardships because of my lifestyle. But God gave me a daughter. No matter what was happening negatively, I looked at her and remembered God – it always brought a smile to my face and heart. I now realize that it was the Holy Spirit revealing this to me. This experience continues to this day. God is so wonderfully faithful; He is the same, yesterday, today and forever!

Because of this journey, I have learned the value of the customs and traditions of the Fantse people. The traditions and customs are all geared towards the prosperity, peace and harmony of community, to support families, to fight against divorce, and to promote mutual respect. A great many of the families that I have come to know have mothers, fathers, uncles, grandchildren, grandfathers and cousins included as one family. Some families consist of grandparents and cousins or grandparents and grandchildren. If one is without a home, they are assimilated into a family. This society has something so precious that we Americans have lost, if we ever had it.

A few years ago, a Ghanaian pastor came to Omega to preach. He preached on the prayer of Jabez and his interpretation was: While I am doing good, let me not do harm. For some reason this has stuck with me and has come alive doing the calling. We in mission must be careful not to offend someone not only out of respect for one's humanity and the dignity of their life, but also because establishing relationship is the way to influence some change. To offend someone causes harm and stops all communication and collaboration.

This notion of not doing harm comes out in other ways as well. Numbers of Western organizations and churches have sent hundreds and thousands of used computers to Ghana. They were sent out of the goodness of heart with the intent of being a blessing. The reality, however, is vastly different. 99% of the computers are inoperable and not able to be upgraded. They sit in public dumps and with no way to recycle or to safely destroy. They are causing a monumental environmental and economic problem. When countries experience unexpected calamities we, from the zeal of our hearts, want to send them various things including water contained in plastic bottles. We don't stop to realize that the aid agencies and military organizations have water tankers. One thing a nation in the throes of devastation doesn't need is more pollution and the resulting problems related to refuse that is not biodegradable, such as the water bottles. Likewise the issue of sending clothing. If we are truly putting our neighbors first, then why donate used clothing that we don't want. We should be giving them the best. God gave His best.

It is better to send cash to the reputable organizations that have a system and the ability to distribute what is needed. For instance, World Vision has agreements with various vendors to donate clothing that is new and unused. There is also already established protocol regarding distribution. **While we are doing good, let us not do harm.**

Becoming sensitized to a new culture (acculturated), I have found that even though I am accepted, I don't totally belong and I also don't totally belong to the American culture anymore. In fact, on my return to the U. S., I go through "culture shock" of being in America and almost two months of adjustment. This "otherness" is a strange place to be in as it makes people I know and love, strangers.

People find it silly and even irritating when I say "sorry" so often. This word is said frequently in Ghana. It is a politeness and courtesy one extends to another. Saying "please" in advance of a question is also frustrating to people in the U. S. where in Ghana it is also an expected courtesy. *I find it quite strange that in the U. S. people find these courtesies to be strange.*

I find that being in a culture does not mean I have to be of the culture just as I am in the world but not of it, as Scripture records. There are cultural aspects I am becoming accustomed to and some I will not. For instance, I am learning to discern when to be "pushy" or not about certain aspects, such as school age children not going to "farm." I understand that when a meeting takes place, then that is the time it was appointed to begin, and not before.

Even while I am being diplomatic and accepting of all persons regardless of faith, there is only so far I will go. For instance, when persons I know who are supposedly Christian equate other traditional deities with Christ, I come against it. I have been in places where in advance of a funeral everyone prayed to God in the name of Jesus and then moments later had a fetish priest pray to a dead chief. In those events, I do some Christian counseling to my Christian brothers or sisters. I am not afraid to pronounce the supremacy of Christ while I refuse to participate in fetish practices.

Notwithstanding, it is necessary to understand the intertwining of the faith in Christ, spirit world and fetishism/animism by many of the people. This closeness to "spirituality" actually affords an easier platform from which to teach the supremacy of Christ and to lead someone to salvation through Christ Jesus. It all hangs on relationship and patient persevering, with understanding and yet relentlessness.

The Mfantseman Municipality and Ekumfi District have a large Muslim population. Most are very happy to interact with Christian churches. Mission work afforded me opportunity to have some in depth discussions with them regarding their faith and their perception of Christianity.

One Muslim friend in particular sat down with me and explained why Muslims don't believe that Christ was crucified. He also argued the point about Jesus being a prophet, but allowed that Jesus was the most powerful of prophets. At the same time he quickly asserted that Christians make Him too powerful. He explained that Muslims believe that Jesus was too holy for God to allow Him to actually die from the crucifixion – in the same breath he acknowledged that Jesus died, but not totally. There is a basic rejection of the doctrine of the trinity – that God is three persons, Father, Son and Holy Spirit. We had a nice discussion surrounding that. My friend also enlightened me that Muslims believe in the second coming of Jesus Christ and that at that time, Islam, Christianity and Judaism will merge to become one world religion.

Another Muslim acquaintance who is Ahmadiyya Muslim proffered that Jesus did not resurrect, nor ascend and that in fact his body is on display at a Hindu shrine in India. At the same time, he said that the difference between Ahmadiyya Muslims and all other Muslims is that Ahmadiyya Muslims believe that the second coming of Christ has already happened whereas other Muslims are still waiting on him.

American Christians have something to learn about spirituality from Ghanaians. We have so many layers of the secular, and possessions that keep us from an abundant relationship with our Creator and from having a faith that can expect all things and dream all things. In Ghana, there is no hesitation about praying for someone's healing and deliverance with the full expectation and confidence that whatsoever a believer prays, it will happen. I have participated in a great many prayers and laying on of hands and have seen people delivered, clothed in their right minds, healed and they walked. How magnificent God is!

There can be no limit in my hope in the people and my faith and confidence in the Lord. Oh, I wish more of us in the U. S. would live among these communities!

CHAPTER 2

A Manner of Speaking
"A word aptly spoken is like apples of gold in settings of silver" - Proverbs 25:11 NIV

Language and the importance of words can really be a hindrance at times. There are critical mistakes that we westernized Christians make in dialogue with other humans about humans while we are conducting a "mission." I will discuss the ones that are the most glaring in my opinion.

"Third World Country" is a term that is casually thrown about to designate a nation needing economic and infrastructure development. This term is actually severely offensive and condescending. It connotes inferiority on an entire people and its genesis is entirely racist. Common sense tells us that there is no such thing as a third world. If there is, where is the second world? No, the phrase is meant to demean and lord over. Most nations in the world do not use the phrase, only we who consider ourselves "enlightened" and therefore superior nations (the United States and those in Europe in particular) speak offensively.

"Human capacity building" is another seemingly intellectual and oh so corporately correct designation. Even relief agencies have adopted the phrase in their programming. The western worldview again has succeeded in convincing the world that westerners, even missionaries are able to create a greater human. Our arrogance overlooks the fact that God has created in every human, capacity. Our aim should be only to assist in a person understanding that they have capacity and to begin confidently expressing that capacity. In Ekumfi Asokwa schools we have adopted a motto based on Philippians 4:13. The motto is "Greatness is in me, I can do all things". Greatness indeed is in every human. After all, is not every human made in the very image and likeness of God?

Imputing poverty. On one of my travels in Ghana we decided to come to a rest stop. Just a small distance away in a lower part of the topography, I saw an enclave. It was extremely neat with two thatched roof houses with an outside shower area. The place was fenced in and a husband was helping to bathe a child and the wife was in the house. I watched for a few moments how they moved about in perfect harmony with themselves, their environment and their way of life. How peaceful and beautiful. As I reflected on that scene, I was reminded about the native people in the Amazon who are living as one with creation and themselves. Perfectly peaceful and in harmony. Happy and healthy – until "modernized" humans interfere and impute poverty where there is none and based on our shallow view on what it means to be rich. It is not until we interfere and inflict our viewpoint that their lives change for the worse. In the Amazon indigenous people groups have been displaced – from a natural environment to an environment of slums, sickness and despair. Once we have "rescued" them, they are indeed in physical and economic poverty.

Thinking too highly of ourselves – The Lord has told us to esteem others more highly than we esteem ourselves (Philippians 2:3) In other words, we are to relate to persons in a way that shows respect to them as persons of dignity, that respects their significant personhood. We have to be careful about not "looking down the nose" when we are walking with and serving humanity that might be impoverished on some level.

I remember a well-respected clergy person describing an entire group of people as "raggedy people from a raggedy town." Grieved as well as flabbergasted are what most adequately describes my initial reaction. This is not a mindset that needs to "serve" anyone.

Another time I was in a meeting where some persons were discussing their short-term mission experience. For much of the time disparaging comments were made about the people they served and the food that was served to the missionaries. It was totally offensive to the persons that they came to serve. The families in many instances had to sacrifice satisfying their own hunger and served the best they could. Can we not appreciate the effort? Can we not love ?

In case we get the "big head" God has given us instructions in 1st Corinthians 1:26-31

> *26 Consider your own call, brothers and sisters:[a] not many of you were wise by human standards,[b] not many were powerful, not many were of noble birth. 27 But God chose what is foolish in the world to shame the wise; God chose what is weak in the world to shame the strong; 28 God chose what is low and despised in the world, things that are not, to reduce to nothing things that are, 29 so that no one[c] might boast in the presence of God. 30 He is the source of your life in Christ Jesus, who became for us wisdom from God, and righteousness and sanctification and redemption, 31 in order that, as it is written, "Let the one who boasts, boast in[d] the Lord." (NRSV)*

CHAPTER 3

Trouble in my way - counting it all joy.

On my 1999 visit, I tried to get some so-called American food at a European hotel restaurant.. On the way back to the Sunlodge, I started getting sick. As the day and evening grew on, I was worse and worse. I realized I had food poisoning. I was hurting so bad and so sick I was afraid to go to sleep. I could hardly hold my head up and was pleading the blood of Jesus, because without Him and His blood covering me, I didn't know if I would see the next day. That same year, I was very sick from carbon monoxide poisoning.

After my visit in 2001, when I arrived in Dayton, Ohio, I was not feeling well and thought I had the flu. I kept getting worse and worse with a high fever, chills to the point of shaking and becoming more and more weak. Trying to shake it off was not working, until 10 days later I was too weak to walk or open my eyes. My daughter, was worried about me, came down to my apartment and called 911. Taken to Miami Valley Hospital emergency, I was given intravenous solution for my dehydration and some sort of sedative because my heart rate was so high, even though my blood pressure was extremely low – 55/45 – I knew I was in trouble. The Pfalciprium malaria had taken root in me and the doctors really didn't know what to do. Pfalciprium is the most aggressive form of malaria and I have been told only about 20% of its victims survive when it has grown to the extent it had in me. An emergency supply of Larium antimalaria medication was brought in from Wright Patterson Air Force Base and then, in walks a doctor who does medical missions in Malawi in East Africa and knew just what to do. He saved my life, praise God from whom all blessings flow!

In 2002, I came down with dysentery and malaria many times and heat exhaustion. God saw me through all these bouts and strengthened my resolve to do His will, as well as strengthened my love for my new friends, comrades and my husband.

In 2004 I was run down and knocked down by a taxi on my way walking toward the Asokwa taxi park. Pedestrians do not have the right of way in Ghana. On this day it was market day in Mankessim and the main road which is really two lanes, became 6 lanes. Walking is always precarious because of the aggressive driving and that day was no different. I was really injured but I had to get on with it and go to Asokwa.

That same month, I was coming home later than I like through Mankessim. I had been with the ADP (Area Development Programme) manager, visiting the other community sites and got into Mankessim at 5:30 p.m.

Normally, I try to get to Mankessim by 4:30 because of the availability of taxis. That day I had to take a private taxi to Dominase and just outside of the town, some guys had put concrete blocks in the road to keep traffic from moving. This is a Muslim section of town and normally there is no problem. People are used to seeing me and they know why I am there. This day, they stopped the taxi and a group started shouting "Get the American." One came around to my side, opened the door and started to pull me out. I started to plead the Blood. The taxi driver said something to him, and they stepped away and let us go.

My comrades and co residents of Asokwa are great and wonderful. Even considering that, it behooves me to be aware of my surroundings and not to forget political realities of life. Even the wonderful Nana had some posters in his house, which gave me pause. One poster shows various pictures of the Iraq war and all of them have arrows pointing to the middle photo which is of President George Bush. The second poster shows scenes of Saddam Hussein's hanging with arrows pointing to the middle photo which is of President George Bush. ***Complacency is not a luxury for me***.

On the home front, people think we should not go into all the world, making disciples. For the most part, American churches are too inward, always worrying about "our own". Incredible, wonderful ministry and service is being done at "home." At the same time we are compelled to do mission work, making the Gospel of Jesus Christ a reality in lives of people – our neighbors – which are in various places on the Earth. Humanity worldwide is "our own".

CHAPTER 4

Partners and chiefs

During the 2001 tour, I was enstooled Queen mother of Asokwa because of my work. My husband taught me the oath which I have to say in the local language. The oath is: "*Asokwa Breku Akwa homfre yie(3 times), Emi Nana Abena Eduabah, I, mosua kyire mi oman de, wofreme anopa, ewiabir, anadwo, gye de mi yari, na se manba, mo to.*" This is repeated 3 times. It means, "Asokwa we are together and together we are strong. I am Nana Abena Eduabah, I, I give my oath to the people. If they call me morning, afternoon, or night, unless I am sick, when I do not come, I violate the laws of the town." Nana means chief and Abena means I was born on a Tuesday. Eduabah means one who makes history. This is a load of responsibility. A Queen Mother assists the chief in maintaining order in the community, in development efforts and in counseling women.

Riding in a palanquin is tough and hot, but energizing and exciting. Paraded through every part of town, I am to show that every part is under my authority and responsibility.

The yam festival in Abeadze Dominase is the perfect display of customs and is full of traditions and pageantry. All the queen mothers and the chiefs are carried on a palanquin with huge drums behind each one. All the state comes out to celebrate, and last comes Nana, the King. Everyone is joyous with dancing.

We sit in state and Nana gives his address to his constituents and to the political representatives.

The chief or chieftaincy institution is one of the examples of traditional rulers in Ghanaian traditional community. The chief's symbol of authority and office may be stool, skin, sword, rods, staff, royal drums, etc. depending on the community.

The Paramount Chief (King) is nominated and appointed by the royal family and approved by the community. After this a private installation ceremony is performed in the stoolroom. Some palace officials hold him up and slowly lower and lightly touch the new chief's buttocks on the stool, three times. He remains in seclusion for about a week or two. This is for teaching customs on how to dance, to talk in public, to wear cloth, to comport oneself, etc. Afterwards he is publicly installed as a chief in a display of pageantry and ceremony. He then swears the oath of loyalty to his subordinate chiefs and people. The nomination, election and the processes of making a chief involves the participation of the entire community.

The chief and his council of elders make laws and amend existing customary laws for his community. He is the administrative head of his community. He distributes state offices to well deserved people. In the former times, he was the commander-in-chief of the community's fighting forces (Asafo). He is the link between his political community and government officials, as well as other visitors. He attends to their social and economic needs. He is the embodiment of the community's unity and stability and maintains the unity and stability of his state and family.

The Paramount Chief (King) is the embodiment and custodian of the people's social values, customs, traditions and history. He directs community development and mobilizes the people through communal labor and financial contributions to build infrastructures.

He settles disputes in and between families and individuals, including land disputes, marriage problems, and divorces. He handles breach of customary laws - thus maintaining law and order - and is the final point of appeal in judicial matters. Nana safeguards and enhances the welfare, security and safety of his people. He serves as the sacred repository of The family's genealogy. Additionally, Nana sees to the ritual cleansing of the ancestral stools and shrines of the state. When taboos are broken, he leads the people to perform purification and pacificatory rituals. Because the chief is considered sacred, his death is not spoken in the normal way. Various expressions are used to indicate the death of a chief.

"The mighty tree has fallen"
"The chief has gone to the village"

All these are said in the local language. Anything in connection with a chief has to be done with excellency, for they are very special and important to the state. No matter who a person is, when one offends a Paramount Chief they need to be dealt with because they are superpowers insofar as traditional ethics are concerned. According to the Ghana constitution, it is unlawful to disobey or insult a Paramount Chief.

Nana Ewusi is an integral part of the ministry. Even though he is not from the Ekumfi traditional area, he is always available to help us through protocol issues, he has taught Rights of Passage programs, and instituted an Africa Club for an elementary school in Dayton, Ohio. Due to the great respect for him throughout Ghana, Nana facilitates many things. He has taught me many proverbs, which I teach in the U. S. and also use when addressing the Ekumfi Asokwa community. *Good beads don't speak. He who climbs a good tree, gets a good push. A crab does not give birth to a bird.*

In 2007 and 2012 Nana was elected President of the Central Region House of Chiefs and in 2009 was appointed to be a member of the Council of State while earning a master degree in Good Governance and Sustainable Development. He currently is Vice President of the National House of Chiefs. He has hosted many foreign student groups including seminary students. He continues to be a mentor for the community of Ekumfi Asokwa. Nana teaches me customs and traditions so that I will always respect the people and the leaders. This helps me be effective, where I would otherwise stumble.

CHAPTER 5

Beginnings (God has begun a new thing. Now it springs forth, do you not perceive it? Isaiah 43:19a)(NIV)

My first journey to Ghana was in 1996. While there, Nyame (God) told me in no uncertain terms that I was to preach the Gospel and to love people into God's kingdom. I met with Harry Reynolds, head of the Ghana rural water project with World Vision Ghana. Our first effort was to repair the non-functioning water pump in Ekumfi Asokwa. I brought some savings with me to get this repair done. Mr. Reynolds instantly informed me that they are a Christian organization, and they serve all people, Christian or not. He continued that if we did not agree with that, then World Vision Ghana did not want my money. I fell in love with World Vision right then and there. He took the money and the first small "seed" project was done.

Mr. Reynolds advised me that he had known about the need for a pump repair.

He advised that the leadership in Ekumfi Asokwa was not attune to participating in the political processes so as to petition the district assembly to do something about it. He was rejoicing that we had come and stepped up to the plate. Since that day in 1996, I have worked on relationship building, not only with the community, but also World Vision International – Ghana and World Vision USA.

1996 was a pivotal year. Not only did we begin this journey with the Mfantseman District, but also I had the high privilege of traveling with Rev. Prathia Hall - an awesome woman of God and soldier who had marched with Dr. Martin Luther King, Jr. To be in her presence and be counseled regarding God's calling, was a highlight of my life!

Rev. Prathia Hall at Cape Coast Castle

The following is a brief history of the Akan from which Fantses derive. According to many sources, the Akan, from which the Fantses in Ghana originated, originally come from the Mesopotamian civilization. Approximately 1800 years ago, according to some historians, the Akan people were living in the Western Sudan, which at that time extended from the Sahara Desert to the tropical forest near the west coast of Africa. Many historians credit the Akan for being the first to recognize one Supreme God.

Many empires flourished and then dwindled on the African continent. These empires were highly civilized with vibrant commerce, codes of law, systems of justice, centers of education, medicine, law, scientists and complex banking systems – long before such beginnings in Europe. The first of these in West Africa was the great civilized empire, the Ghana Empire. The Ghana Empire came into being circa 300 A.D.. Its first capital was the city of Ghanata and then later the capital was Walata, near Timbuktu in what is now called Mali, and lasted until the 11th Century. It was then that the Fantse people migrated from Sudan to Mali and lived there until the beginning of the 12th century. They then came to Tekyman for a few months before coming to the coast to establish Fantiland.

By the 15th Century, Portuguese merchants and missionaries found a well organized form of government, commerce, education and military with the Fantses of West Africa. In fact, according to John Mensah Sarbah early explorers in the 12th and 13th centuries found a vibrant nation of the Fantis, which was organized as a Federation. In his published works, <u>Customary Laws: The work of 1665 relating to the Golden Coast of Guinea,</u> Sarbah states, "This work proves that "in 1481 when the Portuguese navigators and other European trading adventurers first appeared on the Gold Coast, they found an organized society having kings, rulers, institutions and a system of customary laws (a Federation), most of which remain to this day." According to the book entitled, "Short History of Ghana", the Fanti's had become rich and strong and had made many of the surrounding tribes serve them; consequently, they became the strongest of all the coastal nations.

The Mfantseman District is located along the littoral area of the Central Region. It is bounded on the west and north-west by Abura-Asebu-Kwamankese district, on the east by the Gomoa district and on the south by the Gulf of Guinea. The headquarters of the district is Saltpond. The district has a total land of 612 square kilometers. The Mfantseman District is one of the underdeveloped districts in the Central Region of Ghana. The Central region is ranked as worst in poverty levels according to 2009 Ghana Statistical Service. Life in remote parts of the district is characterized by widespread poverty, high illiteracy, poor accessibility to health facilities and high incidence of water related diseases, to name a few. Lack of education due to poor structures, lack of teachers also makes habitation in this district hazardous.

In 2015 the government extracted the Ekumfi Traditional area from Mfantseman District as a new and distinct district, and upgraded Mfantseman to a Municipality.

Now, let's get back to matters at hand. In 1997, I journeyed again to Ghana and I arranged meetings at the offices of World Vision Ghana. Pastor Ward, members of Omega, members of Zion Global Ministries and I learned about their comprehensive program of transformation, which impacts not only any particular community, but also the district and region.

Stepping out of the bus in Ekumfi Asokwa in 1997, tears just burst on my face. How incredible that God would trust me, such an imperfect vessel, to do His work. An immediate love for the people came over me. I wasn't crying because of the dire poverty of the people, but because of the  indescribable love and trust that God placed on me.

We visited the community and exchanged proclamations of dedications and Staff of World Vision began a baseline study of the needs of the village. The problem: Most of the children do not go to school and there is no employment in the village; therefore, the young leave as soon as possible to go into the city, where they continue a very poor lifestyle with little or no future. There is no sustained, comprehensive health

31

and nutritional program in place. There is evidence of rickets and other outward signs of poor nutrition.

For the hundreds of residents, there are only one water pump and one well (which is not a source of clean water). In times of drought, the women have to walk very long distances to get water – water that is generally from polluted streams. This kind of water promotes worm infestation and cholera. There is no sewage system and no place for human waste, which also presents itself with a host of health problems.

In 1999 I traveled to Asokwa and spent several weeks there in advance of a pilgrimage tour. The purpose was to initiate the Area Development Program. I had been in continual contact via mail and email, telephone conferences with the National Director of World Vision Ghana, and Randy Strash of World Vision USA. Finally, we had done all the letters of commitment necessary to initiate an Area Development Program (ADP).

Along the way, I met Dr. Joe Riverson who was the previous National Director in Ghana and whose hometown was going to be included as one of the 3 communities from which we would start the ADP. He said that he had been praying for something like that

In October 2000, I was a participant in dynamic workshops in Ghana sponsored by World Vision Ghana and the Mfantseman District Assembly. The ADP is a catalyst for the Ministry of Agriculture, Ministry of Health and Ministry of Education to be involved actively with the strengthening of the area. In fact, they were workshop participants as well. The programme provides for the assistance with small business endeavors. It provides for the evangelization of the area as well, since the programme is geared to every aspect of a person's life.

The ADP is based on family sponsorship and involves a potential of dozens of communities. Omega has committed to a core amount of family sponsors from its congregation and with others to sponsor fully the ADP. We garnered partnership with other churches, namely, Christian Life Center and Macedonia Baptist Church, (Dayton, Ohio) Tremont Calvary Baptist Church (Columbus, Ohio) Union Baptist Church (Hartford, Connecticut) and Zion Global Ministries (Cincinnati, Ohio).

The first year project was geared to community mobilization, education in getting the residents involved in their political processes, and promoting participation in the project and community ownership. In some cases this means teaching basic tasks of life. The first year includes the building of a primary school building and day care center with an office and library.

CHAPTER 6

Organizing the ADP
God who promised is faithful!

The Mfantseman Area Development Program was the first church initiated ADP and the 3rd family sponsorship ADP in the world thru World Vision. Omega Baptist Church, Dayton, Ohio – an African American church, pioneered this model which is based on church partnerships and which includes in-country missionary work as well as church organized pilgrimages for sponsors to see their families. This model has been replicated elsewhere in the world at another church as it was lifted up as the "new model" of partnership.

I traveled to Ghana for start up workshops for the ADP thru World Vision Ghana. Protocol demands that an influential traditional ruler and elders of the communities, principal stakeholders be present. Included in this is the District Assembly of the Mfantseman District. The Chairman of the week long workshop was Daasebre Kwebu Ewusi, vii, the Paramount Chief (King) of the Abeadze State. He is well known and well respected as well as influential among the people of the region and with all the NGOs. Present was the National Director of World Vision Ghana, Mr. Bismark Nerquaye-Tetteh and Sam Asare, Director of Protocol.

Mr. Tetteh explained the history and vision of World Vision Ghana, the needs of the child and the needs of the family. This program will focus on the family and community. Water, health and hygiene, education, entrepreneurship will be the main foci. The ADP is participatory and community driven.

My own expectation *"A charge to keep I have, my God to glorify, a never-dying soul to save, and fit it for the sky. To serve the present age, my calling to fulfill; O may it all my powers engage to do my Master's will!"* (The United Methodist Hymnal Number 413 Text: Charles Wesley, 1707-1788)

We worked in groups on how to extend the transformational work to the fishing areas and the hinterland; to know more about World Vision to promote the development of the child and family, and the strategy to mobilize the communities. Ekumfi Asokwa has been included as one of the start up communities, because of Omega 's continuing relationship thru my work and because Ekumfi Asokwa is the catalyst for the ADP's birth.

Friends of Family (World Vision Ghana staff) and the families and communities will comprise the critical element for the ADP. Other issues discussed were safety, security, and the selection process of families. The families will be determined by the mothers since some polygamy still exists, even though it is outlawed in the nation.

There were in depth reports from various sectors: District Director of Health - Malaria eradication, Polio immunizations, Bilharzia, HIV/AIDS prevention and treatment, childhood immunizations and TB reduction; Director of Agriculture – better farming and fishing methods, better agriculture supplies, grass cutter farming as opposed to killing wild grasscutters and other bush meat; Mfantseman District Assembly – enforcing laws on school attendance, poaching of bush animals, cooperating with the communities' committees to get things done, community chiefs, elders, Ghana Education Service. They will begin photographing families and getting their profiles.

During the workshops, I went to Asokwa with Sister Dora and Esperanza Ampah to see the original school building which was a victim of the clan leader; it has been bulldozed down by World Vision and a new footer and foundation have been poured by them.

All sorts of things were happening at Asokwa. My friend Julie was due giving birth to her third child. Kobina is praying for a wife. He started a youth Bible study in Asokwa and leads devotions. We began to have a small church group. Rev. Michael Mensah is heading this up.

I traveled to Wli Waterfalls to scope out some new itinerary for the 2001 Pilgrimage tour. How beautiful it is! The Agumatse river and stream is wonderful to wade thru. This will be a great way of including a bit of adventure and beauty to the tour. As well, the caves of Shai Hills and the National Rainforest at Kakum will be great sites.

In general, there was a lot of energy and excitement building surrounding the ADP processes. There have been a series of workshops for the Friends of Family (ADP staff) regarding the sponsorship process, and workshops for the combined project committees, regarding money management and bookkeeping. The ADP Manager provided much opportunity for everyone to learn about this whole transformational program.

There is a core of people at Asokwa who are really committed to the building of the school site and they are working so hard. This school building will be a crown for the community.

The Youth Council is taking serious steps to do things collectively for themselves as well as for the community. They have been really spearheading the clean up of the jobsite and they do so cheerfully. They are wonderful young people with a vision and they "get" the ADP process. Their involvement in their community seems to be challenging some of the old guard to become interested in Asokwa and to do something. I believe that a new leadership will emerge from the youth.

Many of the children go to school hungry. This is because the parents lack certain resources. But within the ADP process there is space for micro enterprise so that the parents will be able to elevate their economic status. Meanwhile, I have been preaching and teaching the growing Omega congregation at Asokwa on the principle of tithing and offering. Tithing and offering is up and some persons who have no money are tithing and offering the produce of the land.

In addition, many of the children cannot afford the exercise books. I proposed that Omega send the funds to purchase a certain number of these books. We can have some on hand for the neediest of the children. The parents will be asked to pay for the books via their helping in the breakfast program and also keeping the school site clean.

The rest of this story is being written, looking back.

When the pilgrimage tour group comes next July, we should have organized a way for the group members to purchase the exercise books for the next school year – 2003. The paper we always bring is the wrong paper for the school children.

This ADP has seen its first year almost at a close. Much progress is being made, physically as spiritually. Medical services are being provided as well as immunizations. More needs to be done and it all hinges on sponsorship. We need more sponsors. World Vision International Ghana is doing a great job and they are so open to our walking alongside the process.

Omega Baptist at Asokwa is coming along well. Rev. Michael has been studying the New Members Manual of Omega and is using some of the organizational methods at Asokwa. the families are well with it. It is the families that support a union as it is the families who are vested in the relationship. In this culture, family and community are everything.

While I was in the U. S., Julie sent word that she has given birth to a girl, named after me, Monica Foster Yakubu. The day she delivered, her husband left her, high and dry. This is a point of shame for a woman in a community. As a result, she has taken the children and moved to Takoradi, the second port city in Ghana. Hopefully she can come back so she and the kids can be sponsored.

After many telephone calls with Randy Strash and World Vision USA, Mr. Sam Asare, and letter after letter, email after email, we (Pastor Ward and I) have decided we are going to go to World Vision U.S. headquarters.

This proved to be an almost fiasco. World Vision wants us to do a family sponsorship ADP as contrasted with a child sponsorship ADP, which came as a surprise to us. We discussed various avenues and strategies and at the end, Pastor was against the whole idea.

After several weeks of coming up with new proposals, Randy Strash and Dr. Joe Riverson proposed something that was a workable, attractive compromise and Pastor said okay to it.

The follow up workshops are taking place April 10, 11, 12 and 13, 2001.

After the follow up workshops, after meeting with the National Director, after meeting with Kwame Ansong regarding the upcoming tour, interacting with the communities and the Omega Baptist Church in Ekumfi Asokwa, I am taking some leave time.

In 2002 I did a 6-month stint in Ghana dealing with ADP issues and taking videos of the tremendous thrust happening in the communities. We partnered with 4 churches to get families sponsored and I need to send them video reports of what their commitment is helping to do in these impoverished communities.

I am also working with the Omega Baptist Church in Ekumfi Asokwa. There has been no baptism thus far and no serving the Lord's Supper. The deacons don't quite know their roles and I am not totally certain that all of them have accepted Jesus Christ as Lord and Savior.

June 4, 2002 – Met with the Asokwa community, Rev. Michael and Sister Ellen. regarding the status of the ADP, the Good News Clubs and the makeshift school classrooms. The children are doing well and are so eager.

The next day I had to go to Accra to sign myself in at the U. S. Consulate for my safety's sake. Had a great reunion meeting with Mr. Nerquaye-Tetteh and to satisfy some protocol issues. Everyday thereafter, I participated in the communal labor and dealt with the school children. I am happy that the elders and chief finally allow me to do labor. I even went to the bush to do some weeding with Julie and her grandmother.

Julie's husband has come back – I guess because of the ADP. The World Vision staff have been working with him to become a viable member of his family and community. He is now partiicpating in the community labor and even gives Julie a hand in the bush. This community labor is hard work. It's not about power tools or cement trucks, everything is done by hand. The work on the school building is coming along.

Part of my days is spent making appointments in other cities with various agencies including the Ghana Baptist Convention. Sometimes they don't honor previously confirmed appointments and the long, hot trips make for a wasted day and a good deal of discomfort.

This Sunday we baptized 20 people in a calm stream, what a joy and blessedness. (Fish were nibbling at the feet – it was really great) We also introduced communion this Sunday at worship service. I preached on Matthew 25:14 and that Asokwa should not bury their gifts from the Lord under the ground by not sending the children to school, by not doing community labor.

At the next service, I preached on 1st Corinthians 3:9 Co laborers with God. We have a part to play. We have to do it. God already has done his part. Eyes have not seen, ears have not heard, neither has it entered into the hearts of people what God has prepared for those who love him.

The next few days prove busy. Traveled to Kumasi to meet with Rev, Ofori of Ghana Baptist Convention - a 7 hour round trip - Although we had arranged the meeting ahead of time Rev. Ofori was not available - am still trying to reschedule. Went to Asokwa to work, Mr. Bekoe picked me up to go to the communities of Edumaafa and Narkwa - spent several hours and did some more filming for Omega and the three partner churches.

On the negative, some parents refuse to allow their children to attend school and to make them to go "farm" with them. Some take their children out of school as they are on their way. The staff and the leaders of Asokwa are constantly chastising them and cajoling them to let the children come to school. This is all part of the educational process,

In the other communities, the women have formed women fellowships. This has not been successful yet at Asokwa. The fellowships discuss various issues and receive information regarding women's right, sexual abuse and spousal abuse. There are plans now for organized literacy classes for adults.

PART TWO

WALK THE WALK WITH ME

Day by day, inch by inch with the same
tensions, frustrations, joys and victory,
and the Lord accomplishes all.

CHAPTER 7

Walk With Me

Come and experience the day-to-day walk and growth in the people and in me. This journey is definitely not for the swift or powerful, but for those who persevere.

"I want Jesus to walk with me. Thank you Lord for assigning me and giving me a journey such as this – a life's journey, not just a trip. But what a trip this is. I want to be in your arms, sweet Jesus.

July 14, 1999, arrived at Dakar, Senegal and praise God, I didn't have to get off the plane for transit. I miss my boys and Lisa already. *"Lord, am I ready to do what you have told me to do? What you have been equipping me to do? I love you Lord, you are my strong tower!"*

On to Abidjan, Ivory Coast – my phobia – but the Lord did not give me a spirit of fear, but of a sound mind and power and love. (my grandson Christopher and I had gotten stranded in Abidjan the year before. My family had to get the U. S. embassy personnel involved for us to get out)

Finally, Accra. So happy to see Bro. Essamoah, a clan leader who we had gotten to know. He was at the airport, but World Vision picked me up and took me to a mission house in the middle of town but not anywhere near to anything. I ventured out to see what I could see and saw "Monica's unisex Afro-European Hair Salon – hmmm—

Went over plans for July 31 and August 1 with Kwame Ansong of Sunseekers Tours. He will be here today. Tomorrow, someone from WV will take me around for provisions before they take me to Ekumfi Asokwa. Will get a couple of dresses or wrap skirts for the village also. Checked into the U. S. Consulate Office. Trying to be wise as a serpent.

July 15 the clan leader provided me escort to Forex bureau to change money and to go buying provisions. Then we went to his house. On the way I saw "McBonald's" fast food place.

Thank you Lord for all your unsearchable riches and grace.

Met with Kwame and made further plans regarding the pilgrimage tour group that will come in at the end of the month. Went back to Essamoah's house He had dinner prepared for me and we ate out on his veranda. It was a feast!! fresh watermelon – a whole one – fried fish (eyes and all) Banku with hot sauce. That was really good. Cherry tomatoes, fried plantains, hot stew and oranges. He has offered me his house if accommodations are not done when

I leave Asokwa. I forgot to pack my hairstyling gel – am having a bad hair day. On to Asokwa, Mr. Asare has spoken with me several times re: the project and coordinating drivers with the clan leader.

"Lord be a fence all around me, help me to be totally yielded to you; to give you glory

July 16 at Ekumfi Asokwa – a lot of work has been done on the school project and the elders house to receive visitors. New water is being installed and the existing pump is again repaired. Children are playing soccer and dancing. But some have deep coughs and one has pink eye. I am told that the flu is going around Ghana because of this unusually wet season. The clan leader took me to Amisano and Amissa beach. The atoll off the beach is beautiful as he said it would be.

I don't know how I will eat. The community and the bookkeeper have supplied the house with various things and are bringing a refrigerator later. They have a propane case range top (it doesn't work).

Essamoah had someone prepare food – it was good – enough left for tomorrow. I don't know about Sunday or Monday. Met Julie Yakubu, who is just a wonderful sister in Christ, she has two small boys, Isaac and Phillip. Unfortunately, the next day I discovered that ants had devoured my food. Oh well.

July 17 – I was blessed to be in the company of Julie and then the project committee. The foundation is laid and filled. The work is so hard – all manual labor. No backhoes, no nothing – back breaking work. The men are grouped and groups rotate the days they work. This is communal effort to the bone. We should take lessons.

The women have taken me as friend and the men in the project have stated that Asokwa is now my hometown. Presently, I am not allowed to do any labor because I am a woman, so I went to the market at Mankessim with Julie. What an experience! Mankessim is a town with a large market. It sits on the main road between Accra and Cape Coast. Ekumfi Asokwa is far from the main road, and after going through the village of Abaka.

I think I have sucked in more pollution than in all the city of Dayton – in one day. My fool camera has malfunctioned and can't be repaired. On my first trip to Mankessim, I went in a vehicle on the road from Asokwa to Cape Coast road. The vehicle had bundles of grass, goats, and chickens riding on the roof. The car was started inside with two wires that had to be connected and a 3rd wire that had to touch the two, which caused the spark to shoot out – and off we went. On the return trip the same thing happened, then the thing conked out. We had to be shoved down a hill so it could start. So much heat, fuel, exhaust fumes to breathe

The second trip with Daniel Sam (Nephew of house owner and certified electrician) was a little better going to Mankessim, but going back to Asokwa, we had the same vehicle as first. We got pushed and shoved but it made it, even the hill to Asokwa.

Called the clan leader on my second trip to Mankessim for him to pick me up. There is nothing here for me to do and I need a new camera. I am afraid that the photos I took are messed up. I told Julie to take the food for me to her family. Whenever I go to Asokwa, I bring a bunch of food for everyone. It is customary that I bring something and I do it with joy.

The day has faded and Essamoah did not come to get me. I haven't eaten in two days. Am surviving on cheese crackers and water. Just as I was talking to the Lord, *"You said you would never leave me nor forsake me"*, Essamoah's driver arrived with a note and some food. *God, who promised, is faithful.* We will leave for Accra at 5 a.m. I prayed for Julie's baby, Phillip who has a bad cough. Talked to Julie about issues that the women may have. She is taking down a list of the women in the village and what they would like to see happen. Daniel and Kobina are very helpful, always pleasant. Everyone gets a big laugh at my attempts at the Fante language.

July 18 – Got up at 4 a.m. to get ready to leave. There is a shower room with a bucket of water. In one shower there was a big, brown spider – went to the other shower. There - a huge black tarantula – reminding me of the classic Anansi. I decided to shower with the brown spider. Choices, choices, choices. *"Lord I thank you for your mercy and grace.*

I came back to Accra and went to Essamoah's house. He is gracious and and wants to feed me, but I don't feel comfortable as his wife is bothered by my presence. I don't need drama or to be poisoned. Plus she is a nice lady and I want to respect her and her place.

I decided to call Kwame from the clan leader's and he will put me up at his hotel the Sunlodge in Tesano. The Sunlodge would become my home away from home. I will stay there until the tour arrives.

Sam Asare, World Vision partner relations, called. He is concerned why I was in Accra already. I explained to him and reconfirmed meeting with him and Nerquaye Tetteh, the National Director. A young lady, Efua, went with me to town to see if the camera could be repaired. No way. So, I bought new camera and film. Will have Lisa to pack extra film with the boys, who are coming on the tour. Yay! Went to a couple of bookstores – for multimedia resource library in Dayton.

July 20 - met with Sam Asare, Mr. Tetteh and Dora (ADP manager for Twifo Praso), who has been so instrumental with Asokwa and also my accommodations at Asokwa. World Vision took me to the Accra office of USAID. I was there to see if I could apply for extra funding for some programs outside of the ADP. It is a fortress with high security checks – under the hood, under the car, security doors all over. All I could get is a brochure and a voice on a phone for me to call back next week.

Today at the Sunlodge I met Phyllis from St. Louis. We went to the cultural center and had fun. Bought souvenir items for people on my list. I am disturbed over the lack of respect and the disdain and ridicule with which some Americans treat the people. Even here at the hotel. In the midst of this shock, I met some students from St. Mary's College in the U. S. They are on a study trip and just returned from a visit to Kumasi. They love Ghana and, of course, their lives are changed forever. God is toooo awesome. .

July 21 - Today I will catch up on my journal and Bible study, meditation.

Phyllis took me to a place called "Frankie's" in Osu – ice cream, bakery and hamburgers, fries, *oooooh.* A very nice place. I have not been feeling well. Started feeling unusually tired on Monday, got chills on Tuesday.

July 22 – I am still not well and don't want to eat. Am feverish, cold and having stomach troubles. I wonder if I have malaria, so I stayed in bed all day. The clan leader and his nephew George came to see me this evening. The clan leader was concerned about my health.

July 23 – left at 5:30 a.m. to Asokwa with Essamoah and George. The road to Cape Coast is being repaired; some is being repaved. Was happy to see Kobina, Steven, and Julie

Through it all God speaks to me *There is no greater love; there is no greater friend than Jesus, my Lord.*

Went to the school site. The mould for the base of the columns to hold the roof have been handcrafted. There is frustration because money to the project account has been slow. I remember last week there was a snafu which was to have been straightened out before now.

Had a good time with the women. Julie got their names, ages and we took photos. We had some song, dance, prayers. Prayed over the water pump and new bore hole.

Essamoah had someone make Kenke (made from cornmeal) the old fashioned way. It was really good, but I still can't eat, still feel hot, especially my head and am off balance. The ride back to Accra was horrible. It took more than 6 hours to get back because of traffic. When we were at what should be 1 hour away from Accra, traffic stood still in the town of Kasoa because of road repairs. We went a few feet and stopped for the next 2 and 1/12 hours – almost to the outskirts of Accra. We ate miles of dust. It was sooo hot. Back in Accra, I never moved that fast to take a shower – I was filthy!

July 24 – Got up late, went to take shower, washed clothes. Am staying put to get rid of the last of this illness. Am enjoying listening to Tesano Baptist Church choir rehearse for tomorrow. I will be there! *It's good to know Jesus!*

The next day, which was Sunday, I went to church at Tesano Baptist church. They were singing "Oh, How I love Jesus". Good preaching and the doors of the church were opened. Then came the you know what (ugh) - the announcements.

I have been watching a lot of good preaching programs – Light House Cathedral, International Central Gospel Church. All these days what goes around my mind is that there is no greater love than from God.

July 26 – Went to get my hair done – to get it trimmed, by a local beauty salon up the street. Turns out they don't know how to do my hair - it is butchered – looks like "who dunnit, and ran", but it will grow. What I enjoyed was the young ladies did not start business and no customer could come in unless they became part of the praise circle, because the whole shop was having devotions – singing and praying. What a way to start the day!

Later that day I went to Labadi Beach Hotel hair salon and got my hair together. *Oooo* Praise the Lord!

Before leaving the Labadi Hotel, I decided to get some "Western" food. On the way back to the Sunlodge, I started getting sick. As the day and evening grew on, I was worse and worse. I realized I had food poisoning. I was hurting bad and I was afraid to go to sleep. I could hardly hold my head up and was pleading the blood of Jesus, because without Him and His blood covering me, I don't know if I will see the next day.

July 29, This morning, someone from the Sunlodge took me to Novotel, I was still woozy and I couldn't open my eyes - still too sick. The Omega pilgrimage was coming in and I have to be there! The nurse at Novotel gave me some medication and some Pepto Bismol and by the time the group came in later that night, I was better. I was full of joy to see everyone from the U.S. and my grandsons. This will be fun until I have to go back!

Another journey to Ghana occurred in March 2000 and a great visit with World Vision. While in Accra on March 9, 2000 I went for a walk along the main road in Tesano and then went to Pastor Quaye's church to meet with some of the people. Sitting in my room at Sunlodge waiting for Pastor Quaye to get me to go to church and my attention came to *The Lord who was speaking with me. He said that I am highly favored. I told Him that I know I am, and without merit, but I am so blessed. It's all because of Him. I told God that I was so glad that He loves me. He replied that He loves me with an everlasting love*

"There is no greater love, there is no greater love." I am singing, *"be glorified."*

I went to Asokwa. The project has progressed slowly. It is very hot and dry, all the water is dried up. I am unhappy about the well that was dug by some other agency. It is very deep and open, so anything can drop into it, it is muddy at the bottom and more than that, a child could easily fall in. There is supposed to be another water pump. Played with Julie's kids, Phillip and Isaac. We went to Mankessim to the market to get food for the house. Julie helps me around the community - she is so full of grace. She has a husband but he does not help her in any way.

A few days later back in Ekumfi Asokwa, I went to the school site to pray for it, anoint it and to cast out all things that would exalt themselves against the knowledge of God. Had devotions. I saw a preacher on TV at the Sunlodge the other day. He was preaching on a grasshopper mentality vs. a giant killer mentality. *I am not a grasshopper.*

Rev. Donna Cox's (Rev. Cox is the Chair of the music department at University of Dayton, and an Associate Minister at Omega) group will get in today. The community was surprised by their visit. Essamoah did not let them know until yesterday morning that she was coming. I told them about who Donna is. The community is doing all kinds of things to prepare to receive them.

Everything is dried up. There is no water for the shower or toilet. No water in the well, and very little at the pump. We made do with bottles of Voltic water. Anansi was there to greet me again this morning at the door to the shower. Nana (chief of Asokwa) is coming today. I am anxious to meet with him.

Prayed for the school at the site and asked for the Holy Spirit to anoint it within and without. Kwesi, Joshua from World Vision from the Twifo Praso ADP team came. We toured the well. It is dry except for some residual, dirty water at the very bottom.

A young woman in the middle of this super hot day had her baby with her at the well, collecting water. I wondered about her story because the women usually go to the well in the morning and the evening. We gave her some clean water. I have learned to be careful with my reactions so I won't offend someone who is in dire straits. People do the best they can. It reminded me about the Samaritan woman at the well, I pray that she felt she met Jesus thru our witness.

Mr. Essel told me and World Vision that when the group left last August, Essamoah "bullied" them into withdrawing the community money for the school construction. Allegedly, he told the community that it was for lumber for roofing. Then he said it was because we, from the U. S., needed our bills in Ghana paid! No wonder he did not show up at Asokwa while I was there and did not meet with me in Accra, either. I guess this sort of disappointment is part of the growing process.

Mr. Essel, the elder of the village and Kofi are so dedicated to the project and have much integrity. Mr. Essel is discouraged by what has been done and is worried that Omega Baptist Church will abandon them. For me, I will pray for the clan leader, but it is hard to maintain a feeling of friendship: the Word of God says that there is none righteous, no, not one and that all fall short.

One thing I am learning for sure is diplomacy and patience. It is somehow easier to be patient in Ghana, than in the U. S. Maybe because I am in the position that God truly wants me in and He loves the people of Ekumfi Asokwa, Ghana, Africa with an "everlasting love."

I had fellowship with the young children and we sang songs together "abamwerie" and "yes, Jesus loves me."

There was a big, horrible accident on Cape Coast Road, which delayed Donna and the gang. But when they arrived they did in a big way. They brought clothes, candy, school supplies. They sang songs for the children and the children to them. They greeted the village one by one. It was great.

Later, I went to Mankessim with Kobina who wants carpentry tools so he can have a craftshop. He wants a family but has no means of income. I bought him start up hand tools.

Back at the Sunlodge in Accra, Pastor Quaye and wife Vanessa are coming this evening and I will go to church with them Sunday. The next day I had a meeting with Sam Asare. We discussed the water well, a new pump for Asokwa and the whole disaster with the school building funds. We both remarked on the dedication of the committee, especially Mr. Essel

I am thinking it is time for us to go for an ADP for this area, as well as church planting. Mr. Asare and I discussed the aspects of the Area Development Program. The priority is water and sanitation, school, and evangelism. Along with that comes entereprenuership, better housing, hygiene, medical services. We have verbally agreed on a plan of action.

Tomorrow I have a meeting with President Rawlings' office. This was arranged by Congressman Tony Hall's office. It was supposed to be with the U. S. Ambassador, but somehow they gave me an audience with the President of Ghana. Pastor Quaye will take me, then I will go to Sunseekers office to meet with Kwame.

March 14 -Met with Jimmy Amissah, President Rawlings' chief of staff. He is a very nice gentleman and gave me some tips as well as encouragement. He asked a lot of questions about Omega and what we hoped to accomplish. He was well aware of the work of World Vision Ghana. He is very encouraged by what we are trying to do. Although I was not able to really meet with the President as scheduled, I did see him.

Lord, you are wonderful, Lord, you are Lord of all.

The leaders of the communities are excited and have actual leadership of the communities. The problem with Asokwa is that there is no real leadership due to the continued absence of the Chief of the town. Mr. James Essel, one of the elders of Asokwa is bearing all of it on his shoulders. He is there at all times at the school building, even sacrificing his time at his own farm which is his only source of livelihood.

Narkwa is a vibrant community even in its struggle with poverty. Education is a big thrust as witnessed by the schools. ADP is helping to enhance the schools and to provide new and adequate school furniture for 1,400 students.

Narkwa has beautiful beaches and shorelines that could be transformed for tourism. It is a beauty to behold. The beaches need to be cleaned up from the debris and KVIPs (outdoor latrines) need to be in place. This can be done by assessing each household so and so many cedis per month, so that it can be someone's job for the clean up and continued maintenance. This will begin to address the needs of tourists and make the beaches even more attractive.

The completion status of the school building at Asokwa is behind that of the community of Edumaafa. Partly this is because the people are farmers and have to divide their time. The building at Asokwa is at lentil and the columns for the porch are ready to pour. Then they will be ready for the roof. The building at Edumaafa is above lentil and they have the columns for the porch. They are ready to put on the roof. Completion for this building is estimated at end of August so that the new classes can begin in the building. At Narkwa, they have many school buildings and are focusing on development of teachers and new school furniture.

Medically, the communities have been dewormed; hygiene has been and is being taught (including brushing teeth). Where there is a health problem the ADP pays for medical treatment. In some cases, this has meant sending the patient to Korle-Bu Medical Center (the premier hospital in Ghana, in Accra) for surgeries. For example, a man at Narkwa had some serious illness with his intestinal tract and had to have two major surgeries to save his life. A young girl had accidentally burned herself severely with a kerosene lamp. The burns were extensive – it burned more than half of her upper torso, left hip, and left her disfigured with terrible scarring. Because of sponsorship, she is being taken to Korle Bu for treatment, including some plastic surgery.

The youth councils are organized to get the youth involved in the community and to encourage them to engage in income producing activities. They have by-laws and their own officers. Some activities include broom making and making pineapple jam for sale. They are also being taught the management of money.

There are 60 children total in the Good News club, Ekumfi Asokwa, so far. Everyone, including the school teachers are evangelizing the children and teaching the Word - it is so exciting to see. Rev. Michael successfully went to classes for Child Evangelism and is leading the Good News club at Asokwa, which meets at 4 p.m. on Saturday.

In general, there is a lot of energy and excitement building surrounding the ADP processes. There have been a series of workshops for the Friends of Family (ADP staff) regarding the sponsorship process, and workshops for the combined project committees, regarding money management and bookkeeping. Mr. Bekoe is providing much opportunity for everyone to learn about this whole transformational program.

There is a core of people at Asokwa who are really committed to the building of the school site and they are working so hard. This school building will be a crown for the community.

The Youth Council is taking serious steps to do things collectively for themselves as well as for the community. They have been really spearheading the clean up of the jobsite and they do so cheerfully. They are wonderful young people with a vision and they "get" the ADP process. Their involvement in their community seems to be challenging some of the old guard to become interested in Asokwa and to do something. I believe that a new leadership will emerge from the youth.

Many of the children go to school hungry. This is because the parents lack certain resources. But within the ADP process there is space for micro enterprise so that the parents will be able to elevate their economic status. Meanwhile, Rev. Michael and I have been preaching and teaching the growing Omega congregation at Asokwa on the principle of tithing and offering. Tithing and offering is up and some persons who have no money are tithing and offering the produce of the land.

Rev. Michael is organizing the congregation to pray and fast, to evangelize and to do community work. I have talked with Ima and will try to meet with Mr. Bekoe in reference to beginning a breakfast program for the school children. This will have to come from the church. As people are increasing their tithing and offering (money as well as produce) the members of the church can distribute the produce via making some breakfast available to the school children. This will take some organization, but it can work and the people will feel good about what they have done.

In addition, many of the children cannot afford the exercise books. I am proposing that Omega send the funds to purchase a certain number of these books. They cost 1,000 cedis(based on the currency at the time) each. We can have some on hand for the neediest of the children. The parents will be asked to pay for the books via their helping in the breakfast program and also keeping the school site clean. I am proposing this also thru the ADP office inasmuch as they need to be informed as well as consulted, and because some organizing will be done by Ima.

When the pilgrimage tour group comes next July, we should have organized a way for the group members to purchase the exercise books for the next school year – 2003. The paper we always bring is the wrong paper for the school children.

This ADP has seen its first year almost at a close. Much progress is being made, physically as spiritually. Medical services are being provided as well as immunizations. More needs to be done and it all hinges on sponsorship. We need more sponsors World Vision International Ghana is doing a great job and they are so open to our walking alongside the process.

One major concern at the present time is the quality of education at the primary level, which I have pressed and continue to press with the Ghana Education Service and the ADP manager, as well as the community. One month ago, Omega Dayton made it possible for me to take the children on an all day field trip to Kakum National Rain Forest and to the Cape Coast Castle. It was the first time they had ever been out of their community. We will be taking them to regularly scheduled field trips when I return.

The issue of the teachers in the Asokwa school is continuing to concern me. School will start on Jan 4 (tomorrow) and I will be there. I have purchased workbooks, pencils and exercise books for the primary 1 and 2 classes and 1 hope to meet with the PTA to urge them to properly equip their children for school. On Wednesday, I plan to go to the Ghana Education Service in Saltpond and get their telephone nos. and email addresses, as well as find out what their plans are,

There are such self-esteem problems here. Specifically, I believe that the colonialism has had a terribly long lasting effect on the people. Even when I preach and teach, I have to remind people that when I say Jesus is Lord, the Lord is not like the English lords of the Colonial period and that all learning and religion and medicine, science as well as philosophy came from Africa.

I am pressing the issue of holding up African and especially Ghanaian heroes. There are plenty of known Ghanaian males but the females don't get talked about much. However, I have been in the presence of the Presiding High Court Justice of Ghana who is a woman. At this writing, the head of the entire Ghana Police force is a woman and so is the head of the banking industry here in Ghana.

I have engaged the Ghana Education Service regarding the upgrading of the educational experience for the primary students. This last visit to Ekumfi Asokwa impressed upon me some things. The children in primary do not have exposure to some resources and experiences which will allow them to excel and compete locally, nationally or globally. In addition, I was impressed that they don't have expectancy of a bright future. What sank into my mind and heart is that some of this is due to the effects of colonialism and generations of not believing in oneself as a worthy human, to accept their significant personhood.

There is quite a bit of education to be done with the parents also as to how to be parents of school children. With that comes a lot of cultural considerations. World Vision Staff, Rev. Michael and I constantly have to stand by the road and argue with parents to send their kids to school. The excuse is the school fees, but I have seen how they spend the money. (September 2005, the government did away with the school fees) I am very much concerned about the functioning of the PTA, teacher accountability and the parents stepping up their responsibilities as well. As well, I am concerned about presenting opportunities to the Asokwa primary school that in the usual course may not be available. To that end I have brought two TVs, tape decks, books and other teaching supplies, supplied by Omega Baptist Church, Dayton, Ohio.

During the month of August the school building was the main focus because the schools are out and so is the Good News Club. The building is going very well and now is ready for the roof. Everything else is down hill from here. The people are so excited about closing in on the finish line! Committees are meeting re: planning when to finish and to have a big celebration at the same time of the festival – with ribbon cutting by Pastor Ward.

The building at Edumaafa is almost finished and there is excitement in the air there as well. Friends of family are working hard with the sponsored families to continue educating them on the ADP process and in particular regarding the educational process for their children. Those that are truly sick are being taken to clinics and hospitals for care. The ADP staff is also planning for preventive medical clinics, such as eye screening and HIV/AIDS prevention programs.

In August there was an undercurrent of a bit of confusion resulting from the clan leader's resurgence in the community at Asokwa. Some people were not there when he took the communal funds which Omega raised for the first school building. They are confused by him because he flashes a few cedis around. As a result, some people, especially the young don't feel they should have to do communal labor. Mr. Essel is allowing me to address the whole town on this issue on Saturday, September 7.

One thing that I value in this Ghanaian tradition is reconciliation. Reconciliation and redemption are always extended to anyone. I myself don't want any reconciliation with this clan leader, but I deeply appreciate the effort to do so. I know Jesus meant this as he said to forgive others as we want Him to forgive us. There is much more forgiveness in a people who the West sees as "Third World". What a huge lesson for me!

After a restful weekend, I went back to Asokwa to work on the school. – It is a holiday and there was no one there. Spent the rest of the week sewing up loose ends with Ghana Immigration, Kwame and Pastor Quaye.

Had opportunity to preach at all school assembly at Dominase and then at Asokwa. Went to Edumaafa to see the progress, then to the Good news club, youth council and Council of churches. All set up because of the Area Development

Program. Rev. Michael is now the Mfantseman President of Child Evangelism Fellowship. He is preaching this Sunday and I am teaching on tithing. I know what a "good measure" is because of the sellers in the market. If I buy one cup or any quantity of anything they add more to it free. One cup, pressed down, shaken together, running over.

June 28, 2002 Collected communion supplies for the Omega Asokwa church, rescheduled teleconference with Mrs. Sweeney (Chairperson of the Sister Cities Committee for the city of Dayton, Ohio) and District Chief Exec., emailed office, sent reports and tapes to Omega. Set meeting with Kwame re: itinerary. This communication is not as easy as one might believe and costly too.

The next weeks my itinerary was full – each day just as detailed as always. I will just summarize.

July 26 To Asokwa – school site to continue the clean up and clearing away

In Asokwa, I resumed teaching on tithes and offering. Rev. Michael organized the congregation into groups for the purpose of fasting, praying, and evangelizing.

Met with Mr. Bekoe at the ADP offices re: sponsorship recruitment strategies and the WV medical team coming to implement a child survival program, funded by USAID and to plan trip to Ankaful and Narkwa for filming the contrast between the two fishing communities. Went to Edumaafa to exchange greetings with construction manager, then went to clinic for malaria injections

During September, aside from participating in communal labor at Asokwa, my efforts will focus also on filming some contrasts of certain ADP communities and my schedule is also very full as you continue to walk with me – daily between all the ADP communities.

Oct. 2 Made arrangements for donation of sheep, mineral drinks, and merry go round

for school. Nana Ewusi VII, has made all the arrangements, including getting the sheep, merry go round and minerals to Asokwa.

Oct. 4 To Asokwa to firm up the town meeting, transport the sheep, drinks and merry go round to Asokwa; held Town meeting as queen mother and spoke on the ADP process and communal labor, Christianity, African festivals, shrines, and honoring ancestors. Even Jesus himself observed the

festivals. Jesus was not European, and no one should make them believe they have to stop being who they are in order to be Christian. No one has the right to undermine what is precious to them.

Oct.7 Taught at the JSS at Dominase re: the importance of reading and library

A pilgrimage group conducted by Omega Baptist Church, Dayton, Ohio, came in November 2003 to officially dedicate the new school building in Ekumfi Asokwa.

The 2003 Pilgrimage was successful by any measure. The purpose of the trip was to determine the progress of the ADP, to make deeper connection with the people of our sister community, Ekumfi Asokwa, to assess the work of World Vision; to learn more and experience more in the homeland, and to document the progress as well as the deepened relationship with the communities, and World Vision Ghana. We also wanted to document the work of World Vision in concert with the people of the communities and Omega Baptist Church, as well as the partner churches, for the purpose of bringing reports to the partner churches, and to promote more sponsorship. The Mfantseman ADP has seen tremendous growth in the communities and the residents.

Two schools have been built. Ghana certified teachers are teaching, Children are going to school and lives are being transformed. Teachers' quarters have been built. New school furniture has been provided. In some communities adult literacy is being addressed. There are stories of elders coming to learn and to graduate from JSS. How wonderful a testimony that is. There are approx. 200 schoolchildren in the primary school at Ekumfi Asokwa, 500 school children in all the schools at Edumaafa, approximately 700 school children in the schools at Narkwa, and approximately 1,800 students in the other ADP sites. Parent/Teacher associations have been formed. School uniforms were provided to those children in the most dire need.

Ribbon cutting by Omega Baptist Church, Dayton, Ohio, to commission opening the new primary school block at Ekumfi Asokwa

25 Bee hive farms have been introduced with appropriate equipment and training. Various families have been trained in tye dye and batik clothing industry. Better fishing techniques have been introduced, and cold storage facilities for the fishing communities have been built or are planned to be built. This serves to increase economic viability for the families and for the communities.

Health Services continue to be delivered. Thousands of people have been dewormed, and have had basic immunizations. Where there is illness, the sponsorship dollars allow World Vision to avail medical services.

Women have been formally trained to be certified birth attendants. Educational programs on HIV/AIDS have been organized and practical ways to extend care to people living with HIV/AIDS has been intensified. Proper means of waste disposal have been implemented in the fishing communities, which lends itself to prevention of diseases. Nutrition education has also been constant. As a result, the red hair (indicating malnourishment) is not as prevalent as before and there is a noticeable increase in the general well-being of the people. Christian growth is apparent - children and families are being evangelized, church leaders are being trained. There are World Vision staff living in each location.

The World Vision staff is doing tremendous work with the people, the parents and children, in all the communities. This was seen in the new spirit and attitudes of the adults and children, and their concept of what transformation is. The new ADP manager, Evelyn Nsiah brings the work of the staff and response from the communities to a new level. She brings a new and more fervent dedication to the cause of the ADP – to enable communities to become self sustaining and to be viable, vibrant communities at the end of the ADP process, which is 15 years.

The children have new insight as well as dreams and the adults are committed to working in community as well as working to better themselves. The staff works on issues as basic as the need to go to school – educating both child and parent.

In Asokwa, they are all looking forward to the next project which is the latrines (KVIP) for the students and teachers. There seems to be more discipline and organization for the community as a unit. This is seen in the active communal labor.

There is a formal protocol system established in communicating with the community and the leaders, which was evident in the customary greetings and welcome of the group and the group to the communities.

The communities are more aware of the partnership of the American churches that has taken place in order to facilitate the ADP, as well as the residents are more aware and appreciative of the sacrifice of the sponsors. Some even carry the photos of their sponsors in their pockets and are proud to show them off.

A unity among all the "stakeholders" has grown (local residents, World Vision staff and Omega). This was evident in the preaching by Pastor Ward at the Ekumfi Asokwa Omega Baptist Church.

The tour participants were also taught more about customs and their meaning, which enlightened our understanding of the working among all the residents, local leaders and World Vision staff.

We presented, for distribution by World Vision staff, several hundred "exercise books" for the use of the school children, as well as pencils. There was a formal presentation of a swing set and seesaw, and formal ribbon cutting and dedication of the new school at Ekumfi Asokwa. Members of the pilgrimage engaged the people in labor and in worship, congratulating the residents at all times of the great job they have done.

CHAPTER 8

I must finish the race set before me

August 4, 2004, I was finally able to get back to Ghana. Ghana airways was grounded by the United States and finally after 3 days of travel, I am back. I am scheduled to preach revival at Omega Ekumfi Asokwa the 3rd week of August.

Night revival at Ekumfi Asokwa.

The wind, like the Holy Spirit, was gently blowing.

Again my schedule is full - ***do you want to go? Come and see!***

Aug 9 Got to Asokwa. Meet with Rev. Michael Mensah re: Revival, community labor, roofing for church. Toured new building sites and meet with acting chief (Nana Bentil) and elders. Spoke regarding community labor and family photos for profiles.

Aug 11 Went to Cape Coast for emailing, and Asokwa to meet with the community one on one (house to house); had worship service, prayed for the sick in the community, ministered to parents of children who had just died (1 from meningitis and 1 newborn baby).

Aug 12 Cape Coast – To see Women's Center and to Asokwa. Spent night at Asokwa and held night worship and Bible study. Prayed for the health and well-being of the residents and prayed for safe deliveries and healthy babies.

All in all things are going well. The acting chief asked me to have a town meeting to talk to the people about communal labor and also being available for the World Vision sponsorship photos. Since then, the community labor days have been expanded from 1 day a week to 3 days a week – Wednesday, Friday and Saturday.

My sponsored family, the Yakubus. The little girl is my name-sake – Monica Foster.

Julie's husband has become a partner and head of household because of the ADP family sponsorship process.

I have been meeting with Rev. Michael concerning the work of the church at Asokwa, the membership, specific Bible Study classes, the invitation to discipleship, and going to Ghana Baptist Convention. In addition, I have been going around the town praying for various people, especially the sick and those who have lost loved ones.

I preached revival at Asokwa August 23rd thru 26 on the subjects of "being alive to God" (Romans 12), "nothing but the blood of Jesus" (Hebrews 9 and 10) "Unless the Lord builds the House" (Psalm 127) and "yes, Jesus loves me." (John 15). The last night we had an anointing service although throughout the revival we had prayer sessions for individuals with particular needs. God brought healing for several children, including one who had had convulsions daily. The last two nights of revival he was leading the children in singing and dancing praises to the Lord. Glory to His Name! One lady accepted the call to ministry, and God richly blessed every one. The first night there were about 60 people, then each night there were 100 or so and the last night for the anointing service, there were almost 200.

People in the U.S. are really sponsoring our families – so much so that additional families have been added on the availability list.

Sept. 1- To Asokwa to deliver the final roofing sheets plus roofing nails to the Omega church. Everyone is very grateful to Nana Ewusi for getting the supplies and delivering them to the Asokwa church.

The rest of my time was also as hectic as before, but instead of having you take laborious steps with me, I will only say that the communities with the exception of Asokwa are finished with their projects. All that is left is the landscaping and the commissioning by the National Director. The landscaping will be done second week in October and the commissioning on November 16, 17, and 18.

At a town meeting in Asokwa, I talked to them about sending their children to school. I recited a Ghanaian proverb that Nana taught me - *if you guide your children to gain their teeth, when you are old they will help you face out your teeth*- that by taking them to the bush instead of to school, they were not guiding their children to gain their teeth. They understood what was meant. At the end, I told them that they had to take care of the job sites for cleaning up and clearing accumulations of soil in the footer and foundations, as well as clean up the school grounds from the building debris; and secure the swing set and see saw into the ground with cement.

When I arrived the next week, it had not been done. This is why the school children (they were there for just a few minutes so as to not miss classes), Omega church and myself did the work. The acting Chief, Nana Bentil is frustrated with the town, he even dug into his own pocket to pay the masons some money to work and they took his money and did not do the work.

The Asokwa Omega church is working to become a member of the Central Baptist Association which is a "Division" of Ghana Baptist Convention. Rev. Michael would have to take a "track" of classes that will be for 1 year on Baptist polity, practices and history. Since the church is not self sustaining, it is characterized as an unorganized church.

I am organizing a field trip for the students who have been consistently coming to school. It will be to Kakum National Rain Forest and Cape Coast Castle, with a boxed lunch. I am doing all the arrangements. This is to reward and encourage those who are coming to school and as an incentive for the others. I have to remember that the community has not been used to school for more than 20 years.

I am eaten up by flies and mosquitoes because of the rain in the evening and morning and then the blazing sun the rest of the day. I am thankful that God is God.

October, 2004

Oct 1 Met with Evelyn (ADP Manager) and attended prayer meeting in Saltpond with the ADP staff. Prayer was lifted up for all nations and all the World Vision ADP's . In particular, HIV/AIDS in Ghana was discussed. The Ghana rate of infection is 3.2%, but the rate in the central Region is 5.5% with Cape Coast at 7.6%. There was discussion about the capacity of the staff to stay abreast of what is happening in their particular communities and how to deal with those dealing with AIDS, especially children who are victims or are orphaned.

Wake keeping started for Nana Ewusi VII's queen mother who died in June. When they say wake-keeping, they are serious. It is from 6 a.m. on Friday, until 6 a.m. Saturday. And the whole town is awake! She was the Paramount Queen Mother and her death is a very big deal. The funeral for the Paramount Queen Mother is a high event.

Oct 5   Met with Evelyn at ADP offices to plan for the landscaping and the

commissioning activities. The ADP office is arranging "learning trips" for 180 students at JSS schools to take to elite academies and universities – Adisadel (premier boys's academy), Wesley Girls School, University of Cape Coast and National College. This is to give them exposure to higher education hopefully to motivate them to stay in school and to go to higher education. Later, I traveled to Mankessim to make copies of the Ghana Baptist Convention material for the meeting tomorrow with the church.

When I met with the deacons of Omega and Rev. Michael we read over and discuss the Ghana Baptist Convention literature. Later I found myself to a garden center outside of Mankessim to buy some plants for the ADP landscaping. I am donating flowers shrubs and cactus as the plants the staff was trying to develop did not germinate.

On coming back home thru Mankessim, I was almost robbed and maybe something more by a group of young men who were stopping all vehicles with concrete blocks barrier and asking for money. When they saw me they started running to the taxi shouting about getting the American and get the American's money. One guy came around where I was and opened the door and started pulling me out. The taxi driver said something to him and he stepped back so I could close the door and they let us go. This is strange for Ghana – and really scary.

There are too many details to describe, it would take volumes.

The rest of the time in October spent time with World Vision on some future collaborations and with the Omega Baptist Church Ekumfi Asokwa on some ministry matters. Confered with Ima re: last cost of transportation of students and the communal labor in Asokwa. They are supposed to dig the trenches for the foundation for the above ground portion of the KVIP.

Oct. 23 I went to participate in the communal work– it did not come on. Met with Rev. Michael re: pushing the church for their belief statement, getting a procedures manual together, financial statements and a checking account.

Oct. 29 Field trip for Asokwa Primary class 4,5, 6, to Kakum National Rain Forest and to Cape Coast Castle. The kids were really excited and on the way coming and going sang some incredible praise songs in Fante and English. At the end they were happy and worn out.

Oct. 30 Met with Rev. Michael at Asokwa to really push him about the belief statement, etc. We will meet with the deacons on next Saturday before the festival. The deacons think that they should be served by the congregation as opposed to serving the pastor, as a result more work on the church building has not come on yet.

Met with Nana Bentil and thanked him for getting the community out to work. They finally trenched out the foundation of the top part of the KVIP. I asked the foreman to bring the cement by Tuesday, because the town is preparing for their annual festival.

Things are going along. I have to find out what the projects are for this fiscal year for the other communities. The World Vision staff is working hard and is dedicated due to their relationship with the Lord. In Narkwa, some people got jealous because of the teachers' quarters and felt that World Vision should build them some houses like that. So a band of them got together and went to the house of the Friends of Family staff, who is female. They broke out all the windows to the house, broke out the street lights and cut the electrical cable to the house, and threatened to rape her. Then they vandalized the teachers' quarters. The people are in jail now and the community is exacting some sort of punishment also because Sis. Evelyn was ready to fold the Narkwa operation. *In the last days there will be perilous times.*

Rev. Michael says that there is a Pentecostal council in Cape Coast that is nondenominational and any church can join. So next week (Monday) we will meet in Cape Coast and go to the council to see what their tenets and requirements are.

I was telling the evangelism director, Sister Ellen, about some of my frustrations and she reminded me that Jesus was rejected by His own, but He still went to the cross anyhow. In the towns are many Muslims and so many are becoming to understand the love of God thru Jesus, just by working alongside them and trying to show the love of Christ. One elder has been such a supporter and exhorter of the work of Omega and World Vision for many years. He loves the church and I have been told that he is wanting to accept Jesus as his Lord and Savior. He is a kind man, who exhibits the fruit of the spirit. This is not my doing, but by God and if we just obey and be faithful to what God has us to do, then His Word works, demonstrated and preached. God is doing some glorious things.

I found out that Asokwa in former times was a hotbed of withcraft and demonic manifestations. Some of that has been evident even when the group was here last November. But through steadfast work and plenty of prayer of the Christians and the World Vision Staff, things are changing.

I am beginning to learning the meaning of being a "living epistle". *I am so thankful that I can hold on to God's unchanging hand.*

November 2004 schedule included continuing participation in the Saltpond beadmaking, tyedye and batik training. Talked to the participants about opportunities and expectations. They believe that if they can get to the U.S. and scrub floors, they can make a lot of money and live well. I had to break that bubble for them. I don't know who is feeding that junk to them and some of it they get from TV.

The next day I had to travel to Asokwa to check on the school and the children in the classrooms. Collected bamboo with Ima to take to Saltpond for the training program (for beadmaking).

Nov. 4 To Edumaafa for zonal meeting of all the ADP communities, the leaders, chiefs, representative students, teachers to discuss what happened in the program year that just ended . Each community gave an assessment according to their viewpoint and the ADP staff gave their assessment. Sister Evelyn told them off about their reluctance on certain issues including allowing picture taking of themselves for the reports to the sponsors.

I gave a short talk on how we feel as sponsors and we get excited about seeing the photos in order to keep sponsoring and doing more.

At Asokwa I went to the "bush" to view the bee hive farms with Ima and Kobbina.

Nov. 6 To Asokwa – meeting with the Omega church on their belief statement – had a Bible study with them on God and the doctrine of the Trinity. We will have another meeting soon regarding Salvation and the Resurrection. The Deacons have to know why they believe as they do in order to teach it to the congregation and also in the face of opposition. They need to be sure before they adopt a belief statement.

Things are going slow, but they are going. The biggest aggravation is the teachers not showing up. The labor has started and some of the delays this time are delays in getting certain supplies from Accra (steel rods, etc). But the people saw the JSS library and TV education room at Edumaafa and it was as if they saw the light of the possibilities that can come about for the communities.

Jan 2 Preached on the gift of Christmas. 7 persons, including 4 children gave their lives to the Lord. Glory to His most Holy name! They will be baptized next Sunday.

Things are coming along, albeit slow. These holidays really slow things down. Have been busy with the Omega Asokwa church regarding the issues as stated above, they are implementing some things.

Rev. Michael and I will go to Kumasi to meet with Rev. Ofori of Ghana Baptist Convention on January 10 and if we can resolve one issue then I believe Rev. Michael will be alright with membership in Ghana Baptist Convention, thru the central office which is located at Winneba. The Ekumfi Asokwa church manual is coming also. I am confident that Omega Baptist Dayton will be satisfied as to our concerns.

These last two weeks I am winding up things asides from the Ghana Baptist Convention and the Asokwa church manual and hope to get a final 2006 trip itinerary from Kwame on the 7th when I meet him in Accra.

In addition, I have proposed a program of various field trips and "career days" throughout the school year. I will be making grant requests of various U.S. ngo's to carry the cost. The field trips would be every two months - for primary 4, 5 and 6; every three months for primary 1, 2 and 3; and twice a school year for the Kg students. The children are bright and eager to learn; I believe they have a wonderful future if we invest into them now.

The field trips for primary 4, 5 and 6 will be to (1) banking locations in Accra; (2) High Court of Ghana in Accra; (3) National House of Chiefs in Kumase; (4) Kwame Nkrumah Park and Mausoleum; and (5) Cape Coast Castle. In addition, I will be asking business people, educators,

professionals, government officials, etc., to come to the school to explain to the children what they do and how education has made a difference for them. In particular, due to emphasis on girl-child education, the many women who are heading agencies will be invited, as well as local businesswomen.

The field trips for primary 1, 2, and 3 will be to (1) Kakum National Rain Forest and Cape Coast Castle; (2) historical sites in Abandze and Dominase; and (3) visit to a substantial citrus farm in Abeadze state. The children will also be visited by professionals, teachers, business people and government officials to explain the value of getting a good education.

The field trips for Kindergarten students will be generally recreational, such as going to an ostrich farm. This is to get the children out of their usual place and to begin experiencing things outside of their community. Upon my request, Sister Vivian Etroo, Director of the Mfantseman office of Ghana Education service spoke to the PTA and the town regarding their responsibilities and assigned someone from her office to do PLE (parent leadership education). I am just praying that the community and parents will gear up and do well for the children (including getting the electricity and cages going for the tv/tape deck). I am also praying for a change in leadership for the Asokwa primary school.

At a subsequent time, maybe in two or three years, I would like to make computers available for the primary students. In the U. S., children as young as 18 months and 2 years are being taught on the computer. Our children at Ekumfi Asokwa are bright and it is to my dismay that lack of essentials is also hampering their development and education. We are losing these wonderful children before they complete primary as very few advance on to JSS. The children in the Kg and Primary 1 and 2 will be taught how to use the computer and the primary grades 3,4, 5 and 6 will use the computers for learning.

This missionary work is lifelong and although it has its negative moments and frustrations, I would not trade the calling God has placed on my life.

I am thankful that Madame Etroo and the World Vision staff are working seriously with the parents and community about how to support their school children. This is a complex issue and the solution is complex as well, but ***I believe that there is nothing too difficult for God and we can do all things through Him who strengthens us.***

CHAPTER 9

Planting and watering a church

God has given me the privilege of working with the Omega Baptist Church Asokwa lending pastoral leadership to the Pastor and deacons. He has also given me the privilege of mentoring a young church, Word of Faith Baptist church in Dominase, whose mother church is in Kumasi in Ashanti Region.

In the beginning there had been no baptism and no serving the Lord's Supper. The deacons didn't quite know their roles and I am not totally certain that all of them had accepted Jesus Christ as Lord and Savior. I have had many Bible studies with them in Asokwa and Mankessim. Each study was directed towards one subject at a time. There was some confusion on the triune God (Father, Son, and Holy Spirit) and that was tackled first until they indicated a good understanding. The next subject was Holy Communion, not only the context and meaning, but also the how-to-do it. The next issue was baptism, what it symbolizes and the commandment to do it. There have been subsequent lessons on tithing and offering and the role of the deacons to assist the pastor and serve the people. Things have vastly improved.

There is no lack of praising God and calling on the name of Jesus. There is no layer of secular and worldly riches coming between the people and God. African Theology locates Christ as the chief ancestor or elder brother. They know their very existence depends on Him and they don't mind giving Him the praise at all times.

I have been meeting with the church re: the belief statement and hammering it out. Bible Studies have been regarding the Trinity, Salvation and the Resurrection (John 3:16, Romans 10:1-13; Luke 19:1-10; Acts 16:16-34; Ephesians 2:4-10) . The next meetings will be Dec 4 - to do the final draft, Dec. 11 - to meet re: the deacons and Bible study, Dec. 18 - Tithes and offerings – setting the tithe apart. If produce is tithed, do a community meal with the food. Also, we will discuss the financial reporting they must keep. Then that following week we will set up the checking account for the church with three signatures required.

So far, there are almost 60 members, including 25 children. The members of the Omega Baptist Church, Ekumfi Asokwa have adopted the following as their belief statements:

The Apostles' Creed. We believe in God the Father Almighty, Maker of heaven and earth; and in Jesus Christ His only Son our Lord, Who was conceived by the Holy Ghost, Born of the Virgin Mary, suffered under Pontius Pilate, was crucified, dead and buried, He descended into hell; the third day He rose again from the dead, He ascended into heaven, and sits at the right hand of God the Father Almighty. We believe in the Holy Ghost, the holy Catholic Church; the communion of Saints: the forgiveness of sins; the resurrection of the body, and the life everlasting.

We believe that Salvation is a gift from God by God's Grace through faith confession on the Lord Jesus Christ. "because if you confess with your lips that Jesus is Lord and believe in your heart that God raised him from the dead, you will be saved. For one believes with the heart and so is justified and one confesses with the mouth and so is saved." (Romans 10: 9,10)

WORK OF THE OMEGA BAPTIST CHURCH AT EKUMFI ASOKWA

Weekly Sunday Worship Service
Weekly Bible Studies
On Wednesday and Sunday
    morning
Monthly communion
Weekly fasting
Each day persons according to
    their day of birth
External Impact
Outreach to serve the elderly in
    the community regardless
of church membership.
Conducting the Good News
    Clubs for all the children in
    the town
Door-to-door evangelism in the
    town

Baptism of new believers

 Here, we are busy roofing the church edifice

CHAPTER 10

Sermons from the Holy Spirit

All the while of doing the work, the Holy Spirit has given me sermon messages. Even if I wanted to delay writing them down, He would not allow it, bringing them to me wave after wave.

THE DIFFERENCE BETWEEN SHEEP AND GOATS
Matthew 25:46 and Psalm 23

In times past, I used to love to see the farm animals at the petting zoo and elsewhere. But now having seen them up close, I have no love for them. Goats go helter skelter, not in groups. The kids get lost.

The adults and babies seem to have no direction. They knock over everything, they destroy people's belongings. Goats are greedy and will eat anything -they eat garbage. Goats bleet – like whining – complaining - get on my nerves. Even in the wee hours of the night when one tries to get some sleep you can count on some goat making enough noise in the night to wake you up. They always have some noise to make.

The sheep stay together in bands. Their babies are with the mothers. Sheep are strong in voice, confident, and don't baa unless they have to. Sheep must be well fed and they are grazing in grass and open areas – not in human areas.

In this text, when the Master separates the sheep from the goats, the Master says get away – you get on my nerves to the goats. Each one will have to give an account - How will you be counted?

Not all is well with the sheep, however. They roam in groups – in places they should not be. On the road in Mankessim, they almost get hit by autos, run into pedestrians in the market and then panic – all in group. I looked to see what was the matter - they are without a Shepherd. A leader they have, but no shepherd.

In Mankessim, they are running in pack. In their little groups, there is a leader, but not a Shepherd.

You see the sheep, and 50% of them are limping away or are hobbling on three legs. Having no Shepherd to guide them they walk a dangerous road. These sheep are without a Shepherd.

But God says that those that know him, that abide with him He will give the angels charge over them lest they dash a foot against a stone

The Lord is my Shepherd – I shall not want (Psalm 23)

His rod and His staff comfort me. The rod of correction steers us into the right path when we wander or bolt carelessly along treacherous paths. His staff reels us in when we have fallen off track.

Yea tho I walk thru the valley of the shadow of death I will fear no evil.

In spite of chaotic traffic, careless drivers, road hazards, my inattention I can walk this life with confidence and assurance.

I will live my life to show a banquet of God's mercy to my enemies, so that they too will call upon the name of the Lord and be saved.

ONE WITH GOD John 17 John 19: 25 – 27

In this passion narrative we see how Jesus wants to treat us and we see how Jesus suffers on the cross. Yet in spite of his suffering -indeed - breaking through his suffering, he focuses on his mother's future well being. It is astounding that in the moment of his human agony he commends with divine love and affection the woman through whom he came - by His own divine power.

He is demonstrating what real relationship is about. The sweet relationship between God and believer -

between the Creator and His creation. It is a relationship which is deeper, higher, infinite, unlike human relationships.

In the narration of John's Gospel, Jesus calls his mother, woman. As much as he loves her as a mother, as much as he is interested in her welfare as mother, his love, his concern is beyond that of human and more connected by her relationship with him Jesus, the kinsman redeemer and Christ. This passage connects Mary the mother of Jesus and the disciple who has been described as closest to Jesus in a divine relationship and this disciple takes her into his own home. This speaks to us today in that through adoption we are made one in Christ and one with Christ; that when we confess Christ as Savior we are baptized into the Body of Christ. There is a relationship that is more eternal than blood, more eternal than a good buddy. You see that there is a greater relationship than human. It is the relationship between God and His Church, between Creator and His creation.

It is a relationship not of our doing but of the blood of Jesus, the heart of God and the power of the Holy Spirit. This love allows us -no-compels us to bear one another's pain and joy. When I wonder if anyone truly cares, I remember that Jesus took me in and has given me a large family I can turn to when I get discouraged I remember that elder brother Jesus has my back. When I feel lonely, I remember that Jesus is the lover of my soul. In my lifetime I have felt despised and rejected but Glory be to God, in Jesus I found the real deal of love and acceptance.

When he gave his mother into the care of the disciple, and the disciple to his mother, Jesus gave us to each other.

I THIRST John 19:28

To quench thirst we turn to various ways of satisfaction.

Are we Pepsi lovers? we have the right one baby. Cola lovers, we want to teach the world to sing; not only to sing, but in perfect harmony. Or, we can kick up our heals, drink Dr. Pepper and be a pepper too.

And for all the hype associated with them, we will be thirstier afterwards. What we need is water.

But even the water in the USA, from our taps is unclean, filled with all sorts of chemicals and bacteria. We constantly see boil water orders for various communities, so we drink bottled water. The bottled water some say is "dead water" and indeed, there have been instances when bottled water hyped as spring water was water from somebody's garden hose. So, the only real, for real, sho' nuff for real water, is Jesus the Christ, who is the living water. But here Jesus himself is thirsting.

After he has rung himself out in the Garden of Gethsemane, been whipped, flogged, tortured. He is in critical condition. His body water and blood is rampaging out of him. In total dehydration, he is in dire thirst, a thirst beyond thirst, desperate thirst. In this hellish condition, he needs a radical refreshing physically and in the spirit

This type of thirst is revealed in the rich man experiencing torments of hell, that begged for a drop of water to cool his tongue and begged Abraham to warn others not come to this hell. This is the thirst Jesus told about to the Samaritan woman at the well, that if she drank the living water, she would not thirst again.

Jesus is about to finish His work. By Jesus thirsting, He quenched the condemnation of our sin sick souls, going even into hell and setting captives free. His suffering includes knowing that His disciples still don't get it. In fact, the majority don't appear to be at the place of crucifixion. Do we get it? Jesus is thirsting for the people He prayed about in Chapter 17, us, those that would believe on Him because of these same disciples that had followed Jesus.

He is thirsting for a people, for a church who would take up their cross daily and follow Him. Thirsting for those who would go into all the world, even the uttermost parts of the earth to proclaim Him, to set captives free, to show our faith by our works.

The reality is that too many of us think we have done something if we break one bead of sweat for our Savior. We find it difficult to sacrifice a cup of coffee or a carton of cigarettes for His name's sake. Just as Jesus poured out everything for us, we are called to surrender it all to Jesus and for Jesus. Our comfort, our very lives. Is He not worth it?

Oh! that we would show our love for Him if we do his Word.

To be parched, to be dried up, dried out, by giving out to others what God has given us. Ministering to the world by lifting up the name of Jesus in every place, at every time, to everyone.

We cannot claim to be Christ followers if we don't do the work and we are not finished with our work until **we** can truly tell the Lord, from the depths of our soul - I Thirst.

HE IS RISEN 1 Corinthians 15: 14-2

Some people in this world are confused about the Resurrection of Jesus Christ. Some say that Jesus was not crucified. Others say that he did not die, that he was in a "swoon" and others even say that there is no Resurrection.

The evidence:

Mary Magdalene had a profound experience with the Lord. When she saw the tomb empty she began weeping, but the Lord Jesus stepped out and spoke to her and called her by name. She just saw Jesus, she knew he was alive. And she knew that he had seen her too.

Seen by 500 – Jesus communed and walked with hundreds of people for weeks after the crucifixion. He had breakfast at the sea. He was not a vapor, or a ghost like Casper the ghost, He had a new body.

Ascension – Jesus ascended into heaven as witnessed by a multitude

Disciples' behavior – at the time of the crucifixion they were scared, hiding and devastated. But when they saw him and after he ascended, they were bold, empowered, going everywhere and even being martyred.

And Paul asks in Chapter 15 vs 30 "Why do we put ourselves at risk?"

If this is a con game, nobody would be willing to give up their life. A person who cons others, does so at the other person's expense, not his own.

The falling of the Holy Spirit. Jesus said that when He left He would send the Holy Spirit. Now the Spirit would not have been poured out on all flesh unless He left. Jesus said that it would profit us for Him to leave, just so that the Holy Spirit would come.

Jesus himself gives witness when he says that He will come again, and that when He comes all flesh will see Him. Well, He can't come again unless He left in the first place.

The Word itself is a testimony that Jesus rose and ascended into heaven. The Holy Bible has been dissected and investigated more than any other manuscript in history, but it still stands. God says that heaven and earth shall pass away, but His Word will never pass away.

Worldly evidence. Historians of the day who did not belong to the followers of Christ, such as Josephus, mention Jesus' death and resurrection. Medical Doctors in the U. S., setting out to disprove Jesus as the Christ totally, became believers. Their statements are that medically speaking, with the scourging that Jesus endured, he was in critical condition before he went to the cross and would not have survived even without the crucifixion. For people to say that Jesus was merely injured and recovered in three days is ludicrous!

Because of the Resurrection of Jesus the Christ, there is victory over death. While Jesus was in the tomb for three days, he just wasn't sitting there twiddling his thumbs, or sipping on tea. He was working. Jesus went into hell, snatched the keys and set captivity free. That is why Paul says, "Death where is your sting, grave where is your victory?" Through the Resurrection we pass from one life to another phase of life. Glory be to His name!

COME AND SEE John 1:43-49

This text, in the preceding verses, begins with the identification of Jesus as the long-awaited messiah, the root of Jesse, son of David, as it was prophesied. Here he is not only being identified and called out as the "lamb that takes away the sins of the world", as he sojourns towards Galilee, he is also calling out his first disciples.

He calls out Andrew who goes to his brother Simon Peter, that Jesus renames Kephas which means rock.

He tells Phillip to " follow me " and Phillip finds Nathaniel.

John 1:46 in the New Jerusalem version the question that Nathaniel asks is, " out of Nazareth? Can any good come out of that place?" in other words, are you for real?

Nazareth is the low of the lowly in the region of Galilee- a town of no esteem, in the southern most hills of the Lebanon mountain range, secluded and isolated from the major trade routes. It is situated in a high valley and overlooks the plain through which caravans traveled, but Nazareth itself was not involved in trade and was not considered an important part of the life of Israel.

Nazareth, on the outside looking in, was a town of ill repute regarding morals and religion, speaking a crude Aramaic dialect. In other words, it was considered to be uncultured according to the larger society. But here is Nazareth, the boyhood home of our Lord, Jesus the Christ.

Here is Nazareth, scorned and out of touch with the mainstream, and Nathaniel wants to know, "can anything good come out of Nazareth?"

I invite you to come and see

"Come" connotes action, to move forward, advance, come out from where you are

See – to behold, look with a purpose, intent

Follow – plunge in, advance with, in comrade with, dedicated to a common cause

When we, Omega, visited Ghana, we went to our sister village of Ekumfi-Asokwa, a village in the remote rural part of the central region of the country, close to the coastline. The home of the Fante people.

Ekumfi-Asokwa like Nazareth, not considered an important part of the life of Ghana, not in the mainstream of what is going on, isolated from the routes of trade and tourism, a town of ridicule, deep poverty - Not only materially, but spiritually, and has a reputation of having been a hotbed of witchcraft and juju (voodoo).

Visiting the Ghana offices of World Vision, we found out that Ekumfi Asokwa was outside of the perimeters of their programs of district and regional transformation. Fallen thru the cracks, despised, rejected, a nothing and nobody.

Few of the dilapidated houses at Asokwa have roofs and most of those roofs have caved in. There is no running water, No sewage system, no healthcare delivery system, the illiteracy rate is high. Most of the people live and sleep on bare floors. Those better off sleep on concrete floors. No nutritional system and no commerce. The women of the community work in the fields from can't see till the hot sun in the early afternoon forces everyone inside. No weekends off. Life is so bad, even the animals have left.

But come and see

The second community is the community of our Young. When I look around and I see the reports on Our young people....see their faces on TV and the newspapers, being arrested for all sorts of crimes, being expelled and suspended - tossed out not only from school, but from families and life, one must ask, and I have to ask, can anything good come? When reports come from all around about low school achievements, about loose lifestyles, profane language, apparent disregard for life, there begs the question "can anything good come?

When teen suicide and violence is a main killer of young people, when we see young people in deep despair, feeling unloved, unwelcome in our communities even in their own families and feeling worthless-Adults working two jobs, going to every conference under the sun, every concert, every bingo game and wine sip - seeming to put more importance of being with the guys or the girls - all at the expense of the young we are to be nurturing - Our young have got to be asking the question, "Can anything good come?" scorned, of low esteem and, like Nazareth not considered important and apparently out of touch with the mainstream of society-on the outside looking in.

Just at the very time that the world proclaims that we also are cast aside, the Word of God in

I Corinthians chapter 1 vs. 27-29 states "but God chose what is foolish in the world to shame the wise; God chose what is weak in the world to shame the strong; God chose what is low and despised by the world, things that are not, to reduce to nothing things that are, so that no one might boast in the presence of God."

And again, God says in Luke 6:20 "blessed are you poor" there are two words for poor in the Greek, one means the working poor and the other, ptochio, means the down and out, means the dispossessed -the ones thrown out of their own communities, homeless. It includes the prostitutes, pimps, those on welfare, those in the soup lines. Blessed, because Jesus ministers forgiveness, deliverance and empowerment. He makes the high mountains low and the low valleys high – only he can truly level the playing field of life.

God has placed an anointing upon the village of Ekumfi-Asokwa. He has delivered the full agency of World Vision International and Omega Baptist Church for the benefit of the community. To transform it through instruction in God's word. Instead of just one village, we, with the assistance of partner churches are able to impact 12 communities in the Mfantseman area. Showing the love of Jesus Christ through nutritional, educational programming, programs for providing infrastructure and commerce. Already we have seen the installation of new, clean water sources, new school buildings, sanitation systems, day cares, medical clinics, electrical power, qualified, certified teachers and the beginning of evangelism –

All the children know the good news – Christ died and rose again for you and me. They really pray and know the authority of the name of Jesus. Even those adults who are <u>Muslim</u>, love the church of Jesus Christ, and are at the forefront of the transformation, and offer prayers in the name of Jesus.

When God steps in, the crooked places are made Straight. When God steps in there is no failure for there is no failure in God.

Ekumfi-Asokwa will be a light to not only to its area, but for the region and beyond. Come and see a testimony for what life in Christ can be Yes! Come and see

When I hear negative reports about the community of our young people I have to remember they are not what they are portrayed in the media. Our young people are wonderful. I just have to look at their eyes and remember that God has created them in his image. The vast majority of our youth are striving to be decent young people, working jobs after school, contributing to their families, going to church, not being ashamed to praise the Lord.

Many young people have signed up to work on mission trips in various towns in Mississippi this summer. In the past years, they have eagerly signed up for and worked in diverse places - the desert of New Mexico. The hills of West Virginia and Tennessee. Youth on mission trips – show the power, authority and love of Jesus Christ. Even for those victimized by the hurricanes and still left wondering if anything good can come, feeling being left out in the shuffle - alienated and suffering, there is an answer.

Come and see and you will see week after week the church of Jesus Christ, led by scores of young people, living out the gospel, and being changemakers in the lives of those injured and displaced. Daring to go beyond ordinary for our extraordinary Christ and His calling to us to go out.

An instructor once said that if we truly follow Jesus the Christ, the world should not be the same and we should not be safe.

In Luke 9:23 Jesus says that if anyone would come after me, he must deny himself and take up his cross daily and follow me. For whoever wants to save his life will lose it, but whoever loses his life for me will save it.

There is an exchange of lives that happens when we confess ourselves to be Christ followers. We exchange our life for life in Christ. The problem is that there are Christians and then there are Christ followers. Those of us who profess Christ in America have the easy-believer syndrome - have become pew potatoes, always looking for some razzle dazzle, giving an itching ear to those who tell us 5 steps for getting something out of God.

Instead of discipling the world, the world has discipled us. A cost-nothing belief. But it cost God everything. His word says to become fishers of men, to go to the highways and byways to be witnesses in Jerusalem, Judea, Samaria and to the uttermost parts of the earth - we are to show our faith by our works

1 john 2: 5, 6, declares that if anyone obeys His word, God's love is truly made complete in Him. This is how we know we are in Him. Whoever claims to live in Him must walk as Jesus did.

I challenge you to go out into the community, unto the ends of the earth being not ashamed of the Gospel, and if you get opposition, wipe your shoes and keep on stepping for Jesus.

I don't want the Lord to catch us asleep so that he won't know us, I want Him to say good and faithful servant.

Relinquish your will to His.

Can anything good come out of Nazareth? The case has been made, the evidence is in. The verdict is Jesus, Jesus, Jesus! Jesus, our Lord, our Saviour, our Rock, our soon coming King! Oh, I get joy when I think about what He's done for me - and when He tells me to go, I go. Where He tells me to go, I go - to the highways, by ways, the alleys, my town, my state, the uttermost parts of the earth.

Can anything good come out of Nazareth? Come and see. Come and see the extraordinary life when we give ourselves over to His Lordship.

PART THREE

JESUS IS THE REASON

This portion of the book is intended to provide insight and practical instruction for the purpose of lifting up the name of Jesus and loving humanity into God's Kingdom through evangelism and mission. Humanity is feeling a hunger that they have difficulty identifying and fulfilling. I believe that the hunger is for relationship with our Creator.

As we see the continued decline of moral compass, decline of reverence and acknowledgement of God, we can see a darkness coming over our planet. God is scoffed and mocked, His Word ridiculed, people are being harmed and destroyed in great numbers and Peter said that in the last days there will be perilous times. Whether these are the last days or not, we can all acknowledge that there is a darkness engulfing this world.

The question is what can we do about it? Are we just going to throw up our hands? The answer is to proclaim Jesus – in word, thought and deed. We can and must lead people to the Eternal Light which is Jesus Christ, our Savior, who alone can satisfy the hunger for God that is in humanity's soul.

There are two main parts to this study. Part I focuses on Evangelism and Part II focuses on International Missions. I am so excited that you have chosen this study and it is my prayer that you will find it to be helpful as you prepare to work in the field of Evangelism and International Missions.

EVANGELISM AND MISSION PRIMER

Evangelism

Bringing the Good News of Jesus Christ.
He who was sent, sends us. *John 20:21*

Introduction

It is important that Evangelism is defined before looking at the various aspects of this subject. Evangelism has been defined in many ways by many scholars over the years but they all contain similar tenants in their definition.

Evangelism is bringing the Word of God – the Good News of Jesus Christ. The term evangelism is rooted in the word "*evangelium*" which means Good News.

What is required? That a person has confessed (professed) Jesus Christ as their Savior and Lord. While this study will also help in evangelizing friends, neighbors and family, it primarily is toward intentional evangelism.

After that works follow. John 14:12

So, after one has confessed (professed) Jesus Christ "what comes next", works follows confession of Jesus Christ as Savior and Lord. John 14:12 reads:

> *"Very truly, I tell you, the one who believes in me will also do the works that I do and, in fact, will do greater works than these, because I am going to the Father." In fact, James compels us to action and lets us know* "*22 But be doers of the word, and not merely hearers who deceive themselves. 23 For if any are hearers of the word and not doers, they are like those who look at themselves[a] in a mirror; 24 for they look at themselves and, on going away, immediately forget what they were like. 25 But*

those who look into the perfect law, the law of liberty, and persevere, being not hearers who forget but doers who act—they will be blessed in their doing." And in James 2, ¹⁴" What good is it, my brothers and sisters, if you say you have faith but do not have works? Can faith save you? ¹⁵ If a brother or sister is naked and lacks daily food, ¹⁶ and one of you says to them, "Go in peace; keep warm and eat your fill," and yet you do not supply their bodily needs, what is the good of that? ¹⁷ So faith by itself, if it has no works, is dead. ¹⁸ But someone will say, "You have faith and I have works." Show me your faith apart from your works, and I by my works will show you my faith. ¹⁹ You believe that God is one; you do well. Even the demons believe—and shudder." ²⁶ For just as the body without the spirit is dead, so faith without works is also dead.."

EVANGELISM

Lesson 1

Commanded by Jesus Christ and empowered by the Holy Spirit. Matthew 28:18-20

There are several reasons why we should evangelize but the most important one above all is that Jesus commanded his followers to evangelize. See Matthew 28:18-20 below:

> *18 And Jesus came and said to them, "All authority in heaven and on earth has been given to me. Go therefore and make disciples of all nations, baptizing them in the name of the Father and of the Son and of the Holy Spirit, and teaching them to obey everything that I have commanded you. And remember, I am with you always, to the end of the age."*

He also provided them with the power to do so.

Acts 1:8; *⁸ But you will receive power when the Holy Spirit comes on you; and you will be my witnesses in Jerusalem, and in all Judea and Samaria, and to the ends of the earth."*

Faith compels us

Our faith compels us to go to the highways, byways and thickets to compel (convince) persons to accept Jesus Christ as Savior and Lord, to join the family of God.

Holy Spirit empowers us, compels us and tells us where to go. Our faith in Jesus has to be rock solid. We are a living epistle as we go out. Works follow our faith.

Into All the World

As you read Acts 1:8 what definition of "all the world" do you see?

_____

_____

_____

_____

What part of the world is represented by Jerusalem, Judea, Samaria and the uttermost parts of the earth?

_____

_____

_____

_____

Witnessing is a tool in evangelism. The Word has to be in us so we have to study daily and ask the Holy Spirit to help us see those things that we don't see, hear what we don't hear, and understand what we don't understand. Love unconditionally; be a standard bearer for Christ.

Before we continue, it is necessary for you to determine your witness: Please describe yourself and the "world" around you before coming to Christ.

_____

_____

_____

_____

What changed in you after you received Jesus as Savior and Lord?

_____

_____

_____

_____

_____

What or who did God use to call your attention to Jesus and your need for Him?

_____

_____

_____

_____

_____

Now that you know your witness and considering Jesus as our example, how would you modify your approaches to persons who are youth, who are farmers, who are burdened down with addictions, etc.? What Scripture would inform you on your approach? (change your method but not the message)

_____

_____

_____

_____

_____

EVANGELISM

Lesson 2

Keep it simple

When people don't know Christ or the world has impacted them and they have forgotten their confession, we have to be simple and gentle. This is a matter of the heart, not the intellect, not of academia. They need to know that Jesus loves them unconditionally.

The person(s) to whom God sends us don't need to know Theology. That will come as they are discipled. Salvation is a matter of the heart. Knowing this we keep the message simple - the spoken message and the message we send with our demeanor and openness.

There is a pastor in Ghana who decided to take congregants to the ocean to evangelize fishermen. He went out on the boats and soon discovered that reading is not so easy when a boat is moving from side to side and being manipulated by the wind and waves.

He also found that the majority of the fisherman were illiterate so even if they had the Bible or written Scripture, they might not be able to read or understand. The pastor decided to teach them the "five fingers of the Gospel." Starting with the thumb and ending with the "pinkie", each finger represented one part of the Good News of Jesus Christ.

Thumb – *I am a sinner and was born into a sin nature*
Index Finger – *Jesus died for my sins*
Middle Finger – *God raised Him from the Dead*
Fourth Finger – *I accept Jesus as my Savior and Lord*
"Pinkie" Finger – *Thank you Jesus, I am saved*

This simple method enabled him to have discussions regarding God who is Father, Son and Holy Spirit. Soon, they were learning the Bible. Eventually the fishermen were evangelizing others in boats and every Sunday they gather together in the ocean and have praise and worship. Simple and profound.

Some years ago, God compelled me to go to a regional transit center for Bible study with whoever I came across. The center did not allow for active religious activity so the Lord showed me that all I had to do was to be ready, open the Bible and sit there. He was doing the drawing. People continuously came to the table for study and prayer. Some became "regulars" while some were transiting from one location to another. It was apparent that some had been in church as kids and some had even accepted Jesus as Savior and Lord. Life had placed layer upon layer of experiences that repressed their experiences with God. Some had never thought about having relationship with God, but all were searching for something. That something was God's love.

As we talked, studied and prayed, the layers started coming down. How wonderful it was to see their eyes light up and their countenance change. Jesus is the light of the world. Through this experience the Holy Spirit continued to impress upon me to keep it simple. It is about the heart.

What is your viewpoint of keeping it simple? Can you give Scriptural reference?

_____

_____

_____

_____

_____

To whom is God sending you? What can you do to keep it simple, yet profound?

_____

_____

_____

_____

_____

PRACTICAL APPLICATION: Using what you know now, plan an evangelistic outing and describe your experience;

what did you use to relate to persons, how were you received, what was your reaction?

Date of outing: _____

Experience: _____

_____

_____

_____

_____

_____

_____

_____

_____

_____

_____

Lesson 3

Know Who is doing the work. It is not you

Sometimes, we lose sight of who is actually doing the work. Below are a few examples to remind us of WHO is really doing the work and what our role is in the plan.

John 5:19 **New Revised Standard Version (NRSV)**

> **19** *Jesus said to them, "Very truly, I tell you, the Son can do nothing on his own, but only what he sees the Father doing; for whatever the Father[a] does, the Son does likewise."*

John 14:10 **New Revised Standard Version (NRSV)**

> **10** *Do you not believe that I am in the Father and the Father is in me? The words that I*

*say to you I do not speak on my own; but the
Father who dwells in me does his works."*

Again, in Luke 10:17-20 it is written,

*"The seventy[a] returned with joy, saying,
"Lord, in your name even the demons submit
to us!" 18 He said to them, "I watched Satan
fall from heaven like a flash of lightning. 19
See, I have given you authority to tread on
snakes and scorpions, and over all the power
of the enemy; and nothing will hurt you. 20
Nevertheless, do not rejoice at this, that the
spirits submit to you, but rejoice that your
names are written in heaven."*

One plants, one waters, but God gives the increase. Read **1
Corinthians 3:6-9**

**PRACTICAL APPLICATION: Conduct another
evangelistic outing and describe your experience; Did
you plant or did you water? To whom did you give credit?
You or God himself?**

Date of outing: _____
Experience: _____

_____
_____
_____
_____
_____

_____

_____

_____

_____

_____

Continuing in our study, consider Acts 5:33-39: The Apostles were brought to the Sanhedrin who had previously demanded that the apostles not speak the name of Jesus. A member of the Sanhedrin stood up and among other things said,

> "*... So in the present case, I tell you, keep away from these men and let them alone; because if this plan or this undertaking is of human origin, it will fail; *39* but if it is of God, you will not be able to overthrow them—in that case you may even be found fighting against God!*"

What is your takeaway of Acts 5:33 – 39?

_____

_____

_____

_____

_____

We can't take credit for anything that God does thru us. The Holy Spirit working in the lives of people makes the difference. Do you agree or disagree? Why?

_____

_____

_____

_____

_____

Lesson 4

Nitty Gritty Strategy

Richard Stearns, President of World Vision USA, in his book "The Hole in our Gospel" states, "We do not coerce. Love was intended to be demonstrated, not dictated, nor to manipulate."

We are to proclaim and demonstrate God's love. We listen to and communicate with people of all ages, walks of life, outward appearance and do not judge. At times we encounter persons who the world would have us to avoid based on the appearance of inebriation or lack of hygiene or whatever. The Holy Spirit reminds us that it is what is on the inside of a person that will defile us, not the outside. Not only that, we are not to judge, only to love and to point someone to Christ Jesus. The Holy Spirit will give us the eyes to see everyone as a valued human being.

In Luke Chapters 9 and 10, Jesus is very direct in his instructions to the disciples as they begin outings to various places proclaiming the Lord.

Detail what he instructed

1. _____
2. _____
3. _____
4. _____

Please explain the importance of these details in evangelistic outings.

_____
_____
_____
_____
_____

Determining communities to whom we go should be preestablished and with time parameters. In the event of many persons, street captains should be appointed. A place for meeting after the outing should be pre determined.

_____
_____
_____
_____
_____

Additionally, we should pray for the Holy Spirit for guidance, for anointing – boldness, discernment. What else should we pray for?

_____

_____

_____

What other logistical strategy should be determined?

_____

_____

_____

_____

_____

Lesson 5

Persevere in the message

"See, I am sending you out like sheep into the midst of wolves; so be wise as serpents and innocent as doves." *Matthew 10:16*

"Blessed are you when people revile you and persecute you and utter all kinds of evil against you falsely on my account. Rejoice and be glad, for your reward is great in heaven, for in the same way they persecuted the prophets who were before you." Matthew 5:11, 12

Persevere in the message. Expect rejection. Know you will meet opposition - sometimes dogs, doors slammed, verbal assaults. This is all part of intentional evangelism. Stay focused on the joy *in* the Lord and the joy *of* the Lord. After all, he was met with all sorts of rejection and opposition, and ultimately excruciating physical pain. All for us.

What is the worst reaction you have experienced thus far to your witnessing to someone?

_____

_____

_____

_____

_____

How did you feel with the rejection?

_____

_____

_____

_____

_____

Studying Acts chapters 2 – 5 presents us with crucial insights into evangelism. The passages highlight the incredible empowerment and power of the Holy Spirit in persevering with the message of Christ in the midst of naysayers and persecutions.

In Acts 2 the Holy Spirit has been poured out and certain folks are ridiculing those who are speaking in foreign languages and accusing believers to be drunkards. Peter stood up to speak. Look at Peter being compelled to preach and declare Jesus Christ.

> *"But Peter, standing with the eleven, raised his voice and addressed them, "Men of Judea and all who live in Jerusalem, let this be known to*

you, and listen to what I say. ¹⁵ Indeed, these are not drunk, as you suppose, for it is only nine o'clock in the morning. ¹⁶ No, this is what was spoken through the prophet Joel:......"

Can you find other Scripture that leads you to the conclusion that we should never be ashamed of the Gospel?

_____

_____

_____

_____

_____

How does Peter's proclamation indicate the Holy Spirit at work?

_____

_____

_____

_____

_____

"Fellow Israelites,[d] I may say to you confidently of our ancestor David that he both died and was buried, and his tomb is with us to this day. ³⁰ Since he was a prophet, he knew that God had sworn with an oath to him that he would put one of his descendants on his throne. ³¹ Foreseeing this, David[e] spoke of the resurrection of the Messiah,[f] saying,......

> ³⁶*"Therefore let the entire house of Israel know with certainty that God has made him both Lord and Messiah,[h] this Jesus whom you crucified."*

We should never be ashamed of the Gospel (Romans 1:16). We should never be ashamed of Jesus in front of people.

> *"Everyone therefore who acknowledges me before others, I also will acknowledge before my Father in heaven; ³³ but whoever denies me before others, I also will deny before my Father in heaven."* Matthew 10:32-33

Has there been a time (a place or situation) when you felt hindered to give a witness of the Lord in your life? What was your response to that situation?

_____
_____
_____
_____
_____

How did the Holy Spirit direct you?

_____
_____
_____
_____
_____

Continuing on with Acts Chapter 2, those in Peter's hearing asked what they should do as a result. Once again Peter stands up and talks about Jesus.

> *"Now when they heard this, they were cut to the heart and said to Peter and to the other apostles, "Brothers,[i] what should we do?"* **38** *Peter said to them, "Repent, and be baptized every one of you in the name of Jesus Christ so that your sins may be forgiven; and you will receive the gift of the Holy Spirit.* **39** *For the promise is for you, for your children, and for all who are far away, everyone whom the Lord our God calls to him."* **40** *And he testified with many other arguments and exhorted them, saying, "Save yourselves from this corrupt generation."* **41** *So those who welcomed his message were baptized, and that day about three thousand persons were added.* **42** *They devoted themselves to the apostles' teaching and fellowship, to the breaking of bread and the prayers."*

Every opportunity we have to speak Jesus Christ, we need to take it. As we go and speak to persons about Jesus, the Holy Spirit gives us the power and the words to speak.

Then we get to Acts 3 where the lame man was at the gate called beautiful. Everyone who saw the man's healing marveled and wondered, including the man himself. Once again Peter stood up and spoke to the people. Peter is letting them know that he is not doing the healing but God is. Once again Peter gives a call for salvation to all in his hearing.

> *¹² When Peter saw it, he addressed the people, "You Israelites,[b] why do you wonder at this, or why do you stare at us, as though by our own power or piety we had made him walk? ¹³ The God of Abraham, the God of Isaac, and the God of Jacob, the God of our ancestors has glorified his servant[c] Jesus, whom you handed over and rejected in the presence of Pilate, though he had decided to release him. ¹⁴ But you rejected the Holy and Righteous One and asked to have a murderer given to you, ¹⁵ and you killed the Author of life, whom God raised from the dead. To this we are witnesses. ¹⁶ And by faith in his name, his name itself has made this man strong, whom you see and know; and the faith that is through Jesus[d] has given him this perfect health in the presence of all of you.*
>
> *¹⁷ "And now, friends,[e] I know that you acted in ignorance, as did also your rulers. ¹⁸ In this way God fulfilled what he had foretold through all the prophets, that his Messiah[f] would suffer. ¹⁹ Repent therefore, and turn to God so that your sins may be wiped out, "……*

Now we arrive at Chapter 4 which describes the persecution of the apostles by the government. They "laid hands on them" and put them in custody until the following day. The good news of that is that the church grew by the thousands at that same time.

> *While Peter and John[a] were speaking to the people, the priests, the captain of the temple, and the Sadducees came to them, ² much annoyed because they were teaching the people and proclaiming that in Jesus there is the resurrection of the dead. ³ So they arrested them and put them in custody until the next day, for it was already evening. ⁴ But many of those who heard the word believed; and they numbered about five thousand.*
>
> *"When they had made the prisoners[c] stand in their midst, they inquired, "By what power or by what name did you do this?" ⁸ Then Peter, filled with the Holy Spirit, said to them, "Rulers of the people and elders, ⁹ if we are questioned today because of a good deed done to someone who was sick and are asked how this man has been healed, ¹⁰ let it be known to all of you, and to all the people of Israel, that this man is standing before you in good health by the name of Jesus Christ of Nazareth,[d] whom you crucified, whom God raised from the dead"......*

Notice that Peter spoke truth to power and let it be known that Jesus is the reason. Peter did not shirk nor give any consideration to the threats being made against them. They did not become paralyzed and as they addressed the

Sanhedrin, Peter spoke, filled with the Holy Spirit. In fact, Peter and John can't help but speak about Jesus. Because of the Holy Spirit, we are compelled and empowered.

Based on the foregoing, list what we should pray for:

1. _____
2. _____
3. _____
4. _____

In Chapter 4 beginning with verse 23 and continuing through verse 31, describe how the Apostles prayed.

_____

_____

_____

_____

_____

Describe the aftermath of their coming together to pray as found in verse 32 thru 37.

_____

_____

_____

_____

_____

As we see in Chapter 5, the apostles went out again to the people and many were added to the Lord, "multitudes of both men and women." (Acts 5:14)

Previously we considered Acts 5:33-39 in terms of knowing who is doing the work. How do the 5:17 -42 passages speak to perseverance?

_____

_____

_____

_____

_____

As a result of all their persecutions and yet steadfastness, Scripture (Acts 5:42) tells us that *"every day in the temple and at home they did not cease to teach and proclaim Jesus as the Messiah"*

Let's recap:

1. Be saved
   Know your witness
2. Know your audience change your method but not the message
3. K.I.S.S.
   5 fingers of the Gospel
4. Know the specific message for each outing
5. Know who is doing the work – it is not you
6. Go 2x2
7. Pray before you go
   Holy Spirit to go before you
   Holy Spirit to prepare others' hearts
   Holy Spirit for anointing – boldness
   DOING IT ON YOUR OWN SPELLS FAILURE

8. Be ready to pray with people for their condition
9. Expect rejection
10. Expect results – seen or unseen
    Be confident in God's word – one plants one waters,
    God gives the increase

SECTION TWO

On Becoming a Missionary

Introduction

As American Baptists, "we understand that mission belongs to God. Mission is God's nature. Mission is universal and indistinguishable from the Kingdom of God."

When we consider Matthew 28:19 the Lord told us to go to all nations, making disciples - that meant to all peoples, tribes and tongues.

Missionaries carry with us a sense of urgency, time is of the essence and time is running out. We believe that all humans hunger for God, and that hunger needs to be satisfied. Therefore, we look for new strategies in exhorting churches to step up and make a difference in this world, to the end that all the earth will glorify God. However, our zeal for God must be accompanied with understanding.

Mission work encompasses many methods including Bible distribution, church planting, public evangelism, schools and pupils – transformational development. Mission work is a privilege, working with others, respecting human dignity and significant personhood, remembering that out of one blood, God made all the nations. (Acts 17:26)NKJ

We do not take on the "God complex" that we are the be all, end all and the knowing of all. We co-labor with God and the people to whom he sends us. There are others with whom we co labor. They are called the stakeholders. First, the stakeholders are the people themselves that reside in communities. There are the medical institutions, educational institutions, political and traditional leaders (local, regional/ state, and national). We form partnerships and collaborations with them and it is the co-laborers who determine the goals. We assist and do not insist. We do not employ "shock and awe" or "bowl" people over to our ways. The most important lesson I ever learned and that which I impart to those who would be sent on mission assignments is that we should observe first, respect others first and appreciate those to whom we are sent. We must know that persons have their own unique way of articulating Jesus Christ and their belief systems. Diplomacy and adaptability are a must.

Missionaries always have the goal of pointing someone to Christ and exalting God.

Lesson 1

The worldview of transformational development includes primarily buildings, schools, roads, bridges and the like. But transformation and development come first in the heart and the mind, not in buildings. Transformational development work allows us to experience the overtaking of God's Word in our life – to learn to esteem others more highly than we esteem ourselves, to be able to see others thru the lens of the Holy Spirit, to begin to understand why and how we are to be living epistles.

Transformation has been emanating or coming out of God forever. The relentless mercy, grace and love of God leads us to true transformation as we develop into who God wants us to be. As we work to assist communities to bring transformation to themselves, we ourselves are being transformed.

Romans 12: 1-2

Question: How do you interpret this Scripture in light of mission service as described above?

_____

_____

_____

_____

_____

Mission work in development is transformational – we become the other and the lesser. God is exalted in all. Mission is a tool to point someone to Jesus Christ and the methodology, love of Christ, and our character matter.

Colossians 3:12 states,

> *"12 As God's chosen ones, holy and beloved, clothe yourselves with compassion, kindness, humility, meekness, and patience.*

Philippians 2:3

> *"3 Do nothing from selfish ambition or conceit, but in humility regard others as better than yourselves."*

James 2

> *"My brothers and sisters, do you with your acts of favoritism really believe in our glorious Lord*

Jesus Christ? [2] For if a person with gold rings and in fine clothes comes into your assembly, and if a poor person in dirty clothes also comes in, [3] and if you take notice of the one wearing the fine clothes and say, "Have a seat here, please," while to the one who is poor you say, "Stand there," or, "Sit at my feet," [4] have you not made distinctions among yourselves, and become judges with evil thoughts?"

How do you see yourself in transformation? What is your motive – are you aspiring to be a servant leader or servant? How are these questions answered in light of the Scriptures listed above? (Colossians 3:12, Philippians 2:3, James 2)

_____

_____

_____

_____

_____

In the next few lessons we will explore what it takes to be a missionary.

Lesson 2

Humility and a Servant Mindset

The Lord has told us to esteem others more highly than we esteem ourselves. In other words, we are to relate to persons in a way that shows respect to them as persons of dignity, that respects their significant personhood.

At some time, I was in a meeting where some persons were discussing their short-term mission experience. For much of the time disparaging comments were made about the people they served and about the food that was served to the missionaries.

Using the passage in Philippians 2:3-5, explain why it was totally offensive to the persons that they came to "serve".

_____
_____
_____

These experiences bring me back continuously to Scripture. In case we get the "big head" God has given us instructions in 1st Corinthians 1:26-31. Here God reveals to us who He is using as His instruments. This is a Scripture that continually informs me just in case I might begin to believe that I am doing something. Surely not! It is God who is doing the work! God is very specific in His description by identifying us as foolish, weak, low and despised, things that are not, "so that no one might boast in the presence of God." "Let the one who boasts, boast in the Lord."

In the Gospel of Luke Chapter 16, there is the parable of the rich man and the beggar Lazarus. At death, the rich man continued in his attempts to lord over this beggar Lazarus, still trying to view himself as exalted and insisting that Lazarus bring a drop of water to his tongue. All the while God had placed Lazarus into the arms of Abraham in heaven. God exalted Lazarus the beggar and lowered in status the rich man Lazarus.

Does this inform you of a different mindset in ministry? Yes or No, please explain

_____

_____

_____

_____

_____

In the book of James, God again speaks to us about being lowly or humble. Chapter 1 beginning with verse 9 we hear God speaking through James,

> *"Let the believer[a] who is lowly boast in being raised up, [10] and the rich in being brought low, because the rich will disappear like a flower in the field."*

Elsewhere in the New Testament there are teachings of Jesus regarding being humble and lowly. In <u>Mark</u> 9:35 Jesus is recorded instructing His disciples who had been arguing over who would be the greatest in His kingdom.

> *"He sat down, called the twelve, and said to them, 'whoever wants to be first must be last of all and servant of all."* In Luke 9:48 it is recorded this way... *"for the least among all of you is the greatest."*

Again going to the Gospel of Luke Chapter 14:10 Jesus instructs us not to be so haughty as to expect the best places, best treatment and best seats. How do you see yourself in an unfamiliar setting?

_____
_____
_____
_____
_____

Luke continues on the theme of humility by the recorded instructions of Jesus in chapter 22:24-27

Restate the Scripture in your own words in your context.

_____

_____

_____

_____

_____

In Romans Chapter 12 Paul unpacks the new life in Christ and the marks of a believer. In verse 3 he instructs that

> "*for by the grace given to me I say to everyone among you not to think of yourself more highly than you ought to think, but to think with sober judgment…*" and in verse 16 "*Live in harmony with one another; do not be haughty, but associate with the lowly; do not claim to be wiser than you are.*"

Based on the foregoing, how can we avoid unintentionally exhibiting arrogance and more than that, be able to place ourselves in someone else's shoes and point someone to Jesus? What experience has made these Scriptures alive in your life?

_____

_____

_____

_____

_____

"A word aptly spoken is like apples of gold in settings of silver" – *Proverbs 25:11 NIV*

Lesson 3

Patience

Eccl. 7:8 declares, " *Better is the end of a thing than its beginning; the patient in spirit are better than the proud in spirit.* "

The missionary Rev. William Sheppard was an African American Presbyterian missionary who was sent to the Congo in the late 1880s and served there for 20 years. He is respectfully remembered for bringing to the fore the atrocities that were being carried out in the Congo by King Leopold of Belgium. His efforts helped to bring down King Leopold. At the time, Sheppard was not allowed to do missionary work without a white person to "supervise". Unfortunately this supervisor succumbed to malaria. Sheppard himself endured malaria 22 times while he was in Congo.

Rev. Sheppard was sent primarily to the Bakuba people in the Congo. When he arrived he found that the Bakuba were very suspicious of anyone coming near and in fact were highly apt to dispatch anyone coming near to their land. After some time, Sheppard facilitated an exchange of eggs for groups of traders in order to come near. These traders were eating so many eggs that the villages could no longer supply them and Sheppard was unable to gain access to the next villages. He then decided to stay at the edge of the Bakuba land and observed that they had acres of banana plantain crops. The nature of the plantain trees is that when the fruit (plantains) are harvested, the trees have to be cut down so they can propagate. William Sheppard moved his camp closer to the communities each time an acre was cut down. At some point the son of the fiercest warrior chief came to find out what Sheppard was doing there. Again, after some time, Sheppard was accepted into the communities. It was then that he was able to slowly build a church and church schools, coupled with bringing the Word. Sheppard's wife joined him later and she also taught the girls.

Interestingly, although the adults appreciated Sheppard and his wife, none of them accepted Jesus as Savior and Lord. It was their children that they were happy to send to church and to school, who accepted Christ.

Rev. William Shepherd journaled that "I grew very fond of the Bakuba and it was reciprocated. They were the finest looking race I had seen in Africa, dignified, graceful, courageous, honest, with an open smiling countenance really hospitable.

Their knowledge of weaving, embroidering, wood-carving and smelting was the highest in equatorial Africa." *Phipps, William E. (2002). William Sheppard: Congo's African-American Livingstone. Louisville, Ky.: Geneva Press. ISBN 0-664-50203-2*

Question: How does this story depict the characteristics needed to be missionary_____

_____

_____

_____

_____

_____

Can you articulate Ecclesiastes 7:8 in light of the work of Rev. William Sheppard

_____

_____

_____

_____

_____

How does Galatians 6:9 apply to William Sheppard's work? What if anything would you have done differently?

_____

_____

_____

_____

_____

How does 1 Thessalonians 5:14 inform you in mission methods? Please explain thoroughly

_____

_____

_____

_____

_____

Give a brief summation of Mark 10:42-45, Philippians 2: 7-8 and Romans 15:1-6 as they relate to missionary mindset.

_____

_____

_____

_____

_____

Transformational development in mission is slow, progressive and most often generational. We need to show the same patience that God shows us. I remember a time when I was upset and impatient with certain goals in Ghana. I complained to a World Vision staff member who reminded me about how patient Jesus was and is, and how he suffered and died for us. I went home, sat on the floor and sobbed. The Holy Spirit did not allow me to wallow, but told me to get up and wash my face. The next day as I set out to the community, all the goals had been met! Without me! Again, God showed me that it is He who is doing the work and to be not only patient, but also confident in what God had assigned.

Lesson 4

Observation (Learner)

Observing and learning are necessary in order to be effective, as we just read in the previous lesson regarding Rev. William Sheppard. We should also not be so ready to assume that people don't know God and can't articulate Him in their context and experience. It is necessary to understand the intertwining of the faith in Christ, spirit world and fetishism/animism by many of the people. This closeness to "spirituality" actually affords an easier platform from which to teach the supremacy of Christ and to lead someone to salvation through Christ Jesus. It all hangs on relationship and patient persevering, with understanding and yet relentlessness.

We must watch, listen, absorb and learn about the communities and persons to whom we are sent without preconceived notions, respecting human dignity and significant personhood.

Observing and doing the local protocols are also essential when going to a community. We must observe the etiquette peculiar to each community, such as elders and leaders. Likewise, we must learn the belief systems and the way of articulation of these systems. This learning requires collaboration with the mission sending agency or church, the local leaders, elders, and the political frameworks as well as government agencies.

How does this characteristic come to the fore with 1 Peter 3:15

_____

_____

_____

_____

_____

In the annals of missionary history there is a story of a missionary group who insisted that young brides wear white dresses to their wedding. The problem was that the color white was associated with funerals in that society.

What would you have done as a missionary carrying the Gospel with you?

_____

_____

_____

_____

_____

Adaptability comes alongside the characteristic of observing.

1 Corinthians 9:19-22

> [9] *"For though I am free with respect to all, I have made myself a slave to all, so that I might win more of them.* [20] *To the Jews I became as a Jew, in order to win Jews. To those under the law I became as one under the law (though I myself am not under the law) so that I might win those under the law.* [21] *To those outside the law I became as one outside the law (though I am not free from God's law but am under Christ's law) so that I might win those outside the law.* [22] *To the weak I became weak, so that I might win the weak. I have become all things to all people, that I might by all means save some."*

This is the Apostle Paul's summation of how he adapts in order to bring the Gospel to all he encounters.

What is the underlying motivation in 1 Cor. 9:19-22 and how does it relate to Philippians 2:3,4?

_____
_____
_____
_____
_____

Adapting also means learning to live in heat, lack of water, lack of communication. In short, we must love Jesus enough to become physically uncomfortable.

Yet, we learn to be content in want and in plenty as Paul describes in Philippians chapter 4

> "*for I have learned to be content with whatever I have. [12] I know what it is to have little, and I know what it is to have plenty. In any and all circumstances I have learned the secret of being well-fed and of going hungry, of having plenty and of being in need. [13] I can do all things through him who strengthens me.*"

Because of this journey, I have learned the value of customs and traditions. The traditions and customs are geared towards the prosperity, peace and harmony of community, to support families, to fight against divorce and to promote mutual respect.

Being in a culture does not mean I have to be of the culture, just as I am in the world but not of it. Even while being diplomatic and accepting of all persons regardless of faith, I am not afraid to pronounce the supremacy of Christ.

Hebrews 3:14 tells us "*For we have become partners of Christ, if only we hold our first confidence firm to the end.*" And verses 35-37 of Hebrews Chapter 10 remind us, "*Do not, therefore, abandon that confidence of yours; it brings a great reward. [36] For you need endurance, so that when you have done the will of God, you may receive what was promised. [37] For yet in a very little while, the one who is coming will come and will not delay;"*

Having considered the foregoing, how do you reconcile 1 Corinthians 9:19 and Hebrews 3:14, Hebrews 10:35-37?

_____

_____

_____

_____

_____

Lesson 5

Love

The first time I came to the community to which God sent me, I was fully washed and showered down by God's enormous love for everyone in that community. All I could do was weep that He would have confidence in me to represent that love. My heart was filled with love for every person there. I know it wasn't me, but God who propelled and prepared me. Although I was sent to bless, I was the one who was blessed beyond measure. It has continued to this day.

So, this is the question. What's love got to do with it? Well, let's examine this.

Love is God's character. God's love is perfect. God has given those who receive His Son Jesus as their personal Savior the ability to love as He does, through the power of the Holy Spirit.

1 John 4:7-10

> *"Beloved, let us love one another, because love is from God; everyone who loves is born of God and knows God. Whoever does not love does not know God, for God is love. God's love was revealed among us in this way: God sent his only Son into the world so that we might live through him. In this is love, not that we loved God but that he loved us and sent his Son to be the atoning sacrifice for our sins."*

Romans 5:5-8

> *"and hope does not disappoint us, because God's love has been poured into our hearts through the Holy Spirit that has been given to us. For while we were still weak, at the right time Christ died for the ungodly. Indeed, rarely will anyone die for a righteous person— though perhaps for a good person someone might actually dare to die. But God proves his love for us in that while we still were sinners Christ died for us."*

Please answer the question of what has love got to do with mission and transformational development? What does it have to do with your transformation?

_____

_____

_____

_____

_____

One day I was in community. It was noon and extremely hot and I came by a water hole that had just some collected morning dew at the bottom. There was a young woman with a baby. The mother had a small plastic sand bucket which she lowered into the water hole and brought up what she could get – dirty water.

What would love compel you to do? To say? How would love compel your facial expression?

_____

_____

_____

_____

_____

How would love dictate to you your reaction?

_____

_____

_____

_____

_____

Interpret 1 Corinthians 13:2-8 in the light of mission and transformational development.

_____

_____

_____

_____

_____

When I was young and attended vacation Bible school, we had to learn a song. "I love to tell the story of unseen things above; of Jesus and His Glory, of Jesus and His love. I love to tell the story because I know 'tis true, It satisfies my longings as nothing else can do. I love to tell the story 'twill be my theme in glory, to tell the old, old story of Jesus and His love." (Author: Wiljan Vriens)

I love to tell the story because I know 'tis true, it satisfies my longings as nothing else can do. I love to tell the story 'twill be my theme in glory, to tell the old, old story of Jesus and His love." (Author: Wiljan Vriens)

In terms of strategy in mission, please list the above attributes in the order you see them being implemented and explain why.

_____

_____

_____

_____

_____

Lesson 6

Transformation strategy

Our aim should be only to assist in a person understanding that they have capacity and to walk alongside as they begin confidently to express that capacity. Establishing relationship is the way to influence some change and to have wonderful conversations regarding God who is Father, Son and Holy Spirit. The industrialist and missionary James Yen devised a development credo based on the quote from Lau Tzu, written in China in 700 B.C.E. – a method for transformational development, which I learned when working alongside World Vision in Ghana -

Go to the People
Live Among Them
Learn from them

I have to put a pause there –

*In order to become one of the community, one must go and live
and learn.*

There are some methods in worship also that we need to learn

- *In Ghana when someone says Praise the Lord! The
  response is Hallelujah! When Hallelujah is spoken, one
  hears in return "Amen."*

  *Something seemingly small is a large step in living
  among the people and learning from them. Sometimes
  I shudder when evangelists from the U.S.. or England
  come in and keep shouting "Hallelujah" in a way as
  to exhort others to shout it. Instead, the evangelist
  is greeted with Amen and somehow the evangelist
  proceeds as if the people have not met expectation.*

- *Also instead of holding "crusades" we use the term
  "meeting." Crusade continues to have a negative
  connotation of a violent act and of oppression.*

Love Them
Plan with Them

*They direct what are their goals, aspirations, and methods and
we listen, and we assist.*

Work with them
Start with what they know
Build on what they have

Teach by showing,
learn by doing
Not a showcase
But a pattern
Not odds and ends but a system
Not to conform but to transform
Not relief but release
But with the best leaders
When the work is done
The task accomplished
The people say
We have done this ourselves!

Now clearly much of this portion deals with the physical transformation in the lives of people. Construction materials and methods are different, school schedules are different, levels of curriculum in schools are different. We learn about the communities by plunging ourselves into the brick and mortar work of development. We might learn how to use insecticidal stain on timbers, manually mix cement, etc.; and these are all things we need to know in order to work alongside. We start with what the community knows and, as feasible and acceptable to the people, we can insert some suggestions – lovingly.

We also learn the acceptable decorum and programming in worship services, so that we can be participatory members of the community. The appropriate means of communication and respecting those in authority are likewise critical. Similarly, we learn by listening to the folklore and to stories.

Try to engage the young people in story telling and explain the meaning in local context and Biblical truths.

A greater aspect of living among people groups is that family groups and community groups consist of relatives, friends, and visitors, which create what one author as published by GoodTherapy.org. describes as "Bridges of Human Network". This aspect of "Bridges" comes into full effect when we talk about spreading the gospel message.

We teach our faith by showing our faith and showing the unconditional love to all and by walking alongside as equals – remember we are to esteem others more highly than ourselves. When invited we share our faith and our witness comes into play.

Read 1 John 2-6; Matthew 5:1-16 and state what you have learned from these Scriptures.

_____

_____

_____

_____

_____

How does Romans 12:9-15 inform you?

_____

_____

_____

_____

_____

Last Things

Micah 6:8 tells us

> *"He has told you, O mortal, what is good;*
> *and what does the LORD require of you but to*
> *do justice, and to love kindness, and to walk*
> *humbly with your God?"*

"The Bible is a missionary Book. Jesus Christ is the father's missionary to a lost world." (*Harold Lindsell, Fuller Theological Seminary founder*) Psalm 72:18 and 19 declare that God's desire is that He be worshipped and His glory known among all the peoples of the earth. That is the true aim of mission. Love is the requisite of this.

Transformational development and mission are a never ending action of God's love. It is not just one project or another, it is assisting persons to see themselves as God sees them and to realize that they are the change agents in their lives and communities. We then understand that transformational development is generational.

God's Holy Spirit keeps us looking forward and beyond. We then are able to see persons created in the image of God with potential, worth and hope. Disappointments come, sometimes we cry but we yet have joy and complete love, feel complete love.

We become the other – We are no longer the same. We are looked on as strangers by "our" communities and we perceive events thru the lens of our otherness. Instead of only seeing with our physical eyes the seemingly insurmountable poverty, the Holy Spirit compels us to see the love, assets and strengths that are present in the people.

A piece of advice I would give to anyone is to be flexible, things usually don't go as humans have planned.

Transformational Development thru mission helps persons to see and take hold of the fact – that greatness is in them because God created them in his image and likeness with capacity. It helps us, no - compels us - to never give up just as God never gives up on us.

Transformational development in mission concerns itself with the transformation of the person as a paramount objective. Having said all that, we never dilute the Word that Jesus Christ is exclusively and alone the way to the

Father. After all, God is Father, Son and Holy Spirit. Jesus taught that no one can come to the Father except by him.

Which leads us back to what we studied at the outset which is our Christian faith and evangelism.

BIBLIOGRAPHY AND REFERENCES

The Lott Carey Legacy of African American missions,
Leroy Fitts, 1977, binder unknown

William Sheppard, Congo's African American Livingstone,
William /E. Phipps, Geneva Press
Louisville, Kentucky 2002

Biographical Dictionary of Christian Missions,
Edited by Gerald H. Anderson, Macmillan Reference USA
Simon & Schuster Macmillan, New York, 1998

Go and Make Disciples, Roger S. Greenway
P R Publishing, New Jersey 1999

Let the Nations Be Glad, John Piper
Baker Academic, Grand Rapids Michigan, 2004

Reinventing Christianity, African Theology Today
John Parratt
William B. Erdmans Publishing Co., Grand Rapids, Michigan 1995
Africa World Press, Trenton, New Jersey

African-American Experience in World Mission: A call beyond community
Vaughn J. Walston, Robert J. Stevens, editors
William Carey Library, California 2002

International Bulletin of Missionary Research, Vos. 17-20 1993-1996,
Overseas Ministries Study Center, New Haven, Connecticut
Global Missions Handbook for African American Churches,
Jim Sutherland, Reconciliation Ministries Network,
www.rmni.org

April 2000 issue of Mission Frontier Magazine

New Georgia Encyclopedia, online
www.georgiaencyclopedia.org

African American Center for World Mission
www.aacwm.org

Documenting the South, The University of North Carolina at Chapel Hill
http://docsouth.unc.edu/smitham/summary

Holy Bible, NRSV

Scripture quotations are from New Revised Standard Version Bible, copyright © 1989 National Council of the Churches of Christ in the United States of America. Used by permission. All rights reserved

Holy Bible

Scriptures marked NIV are taken from the NEW INTERNATIONAL VERSION (NIV): Scripture taken from THE HOLY BIBLE, NEW INTERNATIONAL VERSION ®. Copyright© 1973, 1978, 1984, 2011 by Biblica, Inc.™. Used by permission of Zondervan

Holy Bible NKJ

Scriptures marked NKJV are taken from the NEW KING JAMES VERSION (NKJV): Scripture taken from the NEW KING JAMES VERSION®. Copyright© 1982 by Thomas Nelson, Inc. Used by permission. All rights reserved.

1. *Holy Bible, NRSV*

   a. Scripture quotations are from New Revised Standard Version Bible, copyright © 1989 National Council of the Churches of Christ in the United States of America. Used by permission. All rights reserved

2. *Holy Bible, NIV*

   a. Scriptures marked NIV are taken from the NEW INTERNATIONAL VERSION (NIV): Scripture taken from THE HOLY BIBLE, NEW INTERNATIONAL VERSION ®. Copyright© 1973, 1978, 1984,

2011 by Biblica, Inc.™. Used by permission of Zondervan

3. *Holy Bible, NKJ*

   a. Scriptures marked NKJV are taken from the NEW KING JAMES VERSION (NKJV): Scripture taken from the NEW KING JAMES VERSION®. Copyright© 1982 by Thomas Nelson, Inc. Used by permission. All rights reserved.

4. *The Hole in Our Gospel,* Richard Stearns, Thomas Nelson Publishing, Nashville Tennessee, 2009.

5. *William Sheppard: Congo's African-American Livingstone.* Phipps, William E. Geneva Press. Louisville, Ky. 2002.

6. *Why Bother with Mission,* Stefen Gaukroger, Intervarsity Press, Great Britain, 1996

7. https://www.goodreads.com/quotes/215411-go-to-the-people-live-with-them-learn-from-them

8. journeytoforever.org/community.html

ABOUT THE AUTHOR

Rev. Monika Intsiful received her Bachelor of Arts in Sociology/Public Administration from Union Institute in Cincinnati, Ohio. She accepted her call to ministry in 1996, became an Associate Minister at Omega Baptist Church on April 6, 1997. Rev. Monika earned a Master's Degree of Theology with High Distinction from Trinity Theological Seminary and was ordained through American Baptist Churches of the USA.

Reverend Intsiful was the staff Minister of Globalization for Omega Baptist Church, Dayton, Ohio. Reverend Intsiful spearheaded partnership with World Vision – Ghana, World Vision USA, and the Church's relationship with the community of Ekumfi Asokwa in the Central Region of Ghana, West Africa. As a missionary, she has taught, preached and has been keynote speaker in Ghana. She is a YouTube Bible Study teacher.

Her trailblazing includes being responsible for Omega Baptist's successful development and implementation of an Area Development Programme through World Vision in

Ghana, while continuing to work on several other global initiatives. She continues as mission pastor to Ekumfi Asokwa schools, Ghana. She has been called upon to present on various occasions regarding Africa peace and development initiatives.

Rev. Monika is married to Daasebre Kwebu Ewusi, VII, has one daughter, two sons, two grandsons, and a host of adopted sons and daughters.

To do His will is the only true joy in life.

Greatness is in her; she can do all things
through Christ Who strengthens her.

Printed in the United States
By Bookmasters